Man, Time, and Society

Man, Time,

This volume is one of a series of studies supported by the Office of Social Research of The Equitable Life Assurance Society of the United States.

and Society

Wilbert E. Moore

Professor of Sociology, Princeton University

John Wiley & Sons, Inc., New York & London

Library of Congress Catalog Card Number: 63-15999
Printed in the United States of America

Preface

Time figures more prominently in the world of everyday experience and in the thoughts of philosophers than it does in that intermediate sector of human knowledge, the sciences that formalize and generalize the behavior of men. The social sciences have tended to neglect the way the limits and flows of time intersect the persistent and changeful qualities of human enterprises for reasons that are only partly clear. It is approximately accurate to say that the dominance of "static" models in social analysis has resulted in scant attention to the temporal order of social life. And to the next question, why the preoccupation with static models? it is perhaps justifiable to reply that all analytical sciences tend to perfect their descriptions of elements and observations of combinations before they develop the capacity to observe orderly transformations in the course of time.

The book at hand is a modest attempt to enrich the sociological perspective on the orderly qualities of human action by viewing time both as a boundary condition and as the measure of persistence and change.

A few years ago Professor Arnold S. Feldman and I were planning a book on "Order and Change in Industrial Societies," which is still in process. In outlining the book, we decided to include a section of three chapters dealing with certain basic "conditions" affecting all social systems, though not immune to the effects of human ingenuity and of the unplanned consequences of human action. These pervasive conditions are *numbers:* the demographic dimensions of societies; *space:* the ecological concentration and dispersion of human populations; and *time:* the temporal boundaries of life and the sequential ordering of action. The present book grows out of the circumstances that it fell to my lot to draft the chapter dealing with time, that I found the assignment exceptionally challenging, and that my interest had a particular temporal relation to certain independent developments in the plans of The Equitable Life Assurance Society of the United States. The Equitable Society, through Dr. John W. Riley, Jr., Second Vice-President and Director of Social Research, decided to sponsor types of social scientific research that would be of general relevance to life insurance, though not necessarily oriented to immediate company policies or actions. One form of sponsorship was to be "buying time" of scholars, and my academic interest in time coincided with the company's program and with the availability, on my part, of some of the real commodity during the summer of 1962. Though the general outline of the book was prepared earlier, the major portion of the writing was done during that period.

The Equitable Society also engaged the services of Robert M. Cook, a graduate student in Sociology at Princeton University, for the summer of 1962. His task consisted of the exploration of sources of information concerning the social aspects of time, including a systematic search of the Human Relations Area Files with respect mainly to nonliterate societies. He also tracked and checked other sources. His work made a "fast" book feasible, and I am grateful both to him and to the Society for his assistance.

In revising the original manuscript for publication I have had the benefit of comments and criticism by Dr. Riley and by Professor Charles H. Page. As these esteemed scholars are also my enduring friends, I am doubly happy to record my gratitude to them.

While this book was in the final preparation for publication, a book by Professor R. M. MacIver, *The Challenge of the Passing Years: My Encounter with Time* (New York: Trident Press, Simon and Shuster, 1962) was released. The attentive reader familiar with Professor MacIver's brilliant and sensitive treatment will find some parallels with my independently developed discussion, especially in my second and third chapters on individual time patterns. I could not faithfully record in footnotes all of the points of similarity, but I do take some comfort from the correspondence in perspective that here and there appears, while wryly noting that by his superior timing he has preempted some of my favorite ideas.

Since my colleague Professor Morroe Berger published a playful piece on the styles of prefaces I have been uneasy about the forms for recording thanks to one's wife, who conventionally comes at the end of the author's honors list. Let me, then, simply note that Jeanne Yates Moore typed the entire manuscript of this study without notable psychic damage and add wholeheartedly that she enriches each passing moment of my life.

WILBERT E. MOORE

Princeton, New Jersey
March 1963

Contents

I

Introduction

One

The Temporal Dimensions
of Social Life

A commuter, hurriedly stuffing his attaché case, glances nervously at his watch and hopes that no telephone call or personal conversation will prevent his catching the 5:15 train for home. He is lucky, and, once aboard the train, he reflects once more on the two-and-a-half hours spent traveling to and from work, which is the temporal penalty he pays for a decision to live in the suburbs. He does not "waste" all this time, by some criteria of value, but he does note that he would prefer more time with his family and less riding on a train.

During the day he had been engaged in formulating an annual budget for his department in a business corporation. That budget, if approved, will determine the flow of funds to his unit for the next year. His written justification for the requested money had to explain deviations from past practice and trends and from the ten-year plan of the company as applied to his department.

Also during the day his life-insurance agent had reminded him that he had only twenty-five years plus a few months before reaching the mandatory retirement age in his company. By insistent probing he had extracted from the agent his remaining "life expectancy," that is, the average number of years that a person of his age of 40 might live until death. The conversation, depressing at best, had set off a train of thought about his promotional prospects before retirement, his income and activity on retirement, and his obligations to himself and his dependents.

The commuter's wife had had a "leisurely" existence that day. She had called the serviceman to fix the automatic dishwasher, agreed to be home at a specified time, and waited impatiently when, in fact, he did not arrive as promised. She then hurriedly shopped after the serviceman had called and left, only to return "later" with a new part. Home again barely ahead of the school bus delivering her children, she had negotiated with them about homework and television-watching time, had got the dinner started, and fixed up a bit before her husband arrived.

The day being Thursday, the wife was scheduled for her weekly bridge club in the evening. Being the third Thursday of the month, the weary, but alcoholically refreshed and well-fed, commuter was supposed to attend the men's Bible study class at his church. Both, having no superseding obligations, did in fact keep their standing commitments, but each found that part of the "expected" group had one or another competing claims on time.

In the grand sweep of human history the small temporal concerns are trivial and indeed come close to the thin edge of banality. These vignettes of experience, readily recognizable to anyone with more than a smattering of literacy, form the *mise en scène* for magazine fiction, and, with slightly more austere lines and language, the setting for tendentious treatises on American business, family, recreation, voluntary associations, and, God save the mark, national character.

In the world of common-sense experience the only close rival of money as a pervasive and awkward scarcity is time. Loyalty or affection, too, turns out to be a universal scarcity upon close examination, but, for most people most of the time, time and treasure present themselves more insistently as scarce and valuable elements in the basic problems of human existence.

Although time and treasure are somewhat interchangeable, in that either is a potential instrument for increasing the other, the aphoristic equation "time is money" is not uniformly sound. In contemporary American society (and, indeed, in other prosperous and pluralistic societies) time may have small or negative value for the rich, who need not work, and for the poor, who cannot work because they are unemployable or, in any event, unemployed. Though time is scarce for most people in a relative sense, and, given man's mortality, for all people in an absolute sense, any individual may at times experience plethora or surfeit.

Time has intrigued philosophers, at least since persons of a speculative disposition left any records, and conceptions of time are distinctly variable from one culture to another. Yet the temporal ordering of social behavior has received only sporadic or intermittent attention by the sciences dealing with man. Man's numbers and their distribution in space have produced recognized fields of scientific specialization: demography and human ecology. Incidentally, specialists in these fields have considered time as a condition or as a variable to a far greater degree than have other social scientists. The focus on time as a central feature of order and sequence, however, is so minimally developed that no one has even invented a name for a science of the temporal dimensions of social life. (The term "chronology" has been preempted for the ordering and dating of past events and thus excludes the rhythms and cycles, the speed and direction, the strains in time allocations, and the strategies of planning that mark the phenomena of time in human experience.) Our theme is man and time: inventing some designation like "anthropochronology" seems scarcely necessary and, indeed, more than slightly pretentious. Our task is to attend to the significance of temporal scarcity and to the significance of temporal sequence in the social ordering of man's behavior.

Finite Time: The Ultimate Scarcity

Though the concept of time is essentially meaningless unless it denotes recurrence and sequence, a "flow" of distinguishable events, for many aspects of human experience and for many purposes of analysis time may be regarded as fixed, a "static," condition or parameter of behavior. The diurnal cycle is limited, whatever the division into intervals. The same is true of the week (an arbitrary temporal unit like the hour or minute), the month, and the year. Intense activity may conserve time, but only within stringent limits. Over a longer period, it is man's mortality that makes of time the ultimate scarcity. Accumulation and storage are, in the strict sense, impossible, although certain kinds of time claims may be credited: for example, when an employee is permitted to accumulate sick leave or paid vacations. Time lost is never truly regained, although the effects of loss may be compensated by greater intensity of use.

The essence of time is rhythm and recurrence, according to A. N. Whitehead.[1] The *sense* of time, however, might not occur from purely repetitive cycles. Richard Schlegel[2] argues that *change* therefore is also an essential component of temporal conceptions.

It is the finite length of cycles that constrains activity and makes allocation and priorities essential. In human physiology the natural cycles range from the pulse and breathing (and even shorter unlearned timing mechanisms) through waking and sleeping, eating and elimination, conception and childbirth to the prolonged process of growing and dying.[3] These cycles are somewhat peculiar to individuals and somewhat affected by events, but the limits on length of various cycles are fairly severe.

Perhaps the most nearly universal, and in a sense most "natural," temporal unit combines physiology and astronomy: the physiological need for sleep and the earth's rotation to produce day and night. There is a somewhat similar but more remote connection between the lunar months and the female menstrual cycle. The solar seasons also affect a majority of the world's population, leading to some approximations of a "yearly" cycle divided into several recurrent seasonal segments. Age, too, though perhaps not precisely "measured" in astronomical terms, has at least gross physiological attributes that change in all places other than Shangri-La.

The sense of time and its constraints are thus intrinsic to the human condition. The units by which it is divided are always likely to have some biological or environmental basis, but only in part, for any temporal unit based on one kind of cycle (for example, the movement of a minute hand around the face of a clock) may be arbitrary from other points of view (for example, the interest that makes time fly or the boredom that makes it drag). The seven-day week is a purely cultural convention, although cycles of several days of "ordinary" activity set apart by one or more days of recreation or rest are sufficiently common to raise the speculation that a weekly as well as a daily change of pace may have physiological foundations.

Biological time, defined for example by the healing of a wound,[4] may have differing clock values in astronomical time. *Psychological* (or subjective) *time,* though disciplined by conventional or objective time, may still be affected by the individual's interest or boredom.[5] *Social time,*[6] defined for example by the completion of certain kinds of contests, may be similarly variable with regard to hours and minutes. Again, it is recurrence that permits identification of the common elements and the marking off of one cycle from another.

To repeat, temporal units, however identified, are finite. (The escape from such constraints in "eternity" is a theological conception that is one of the most difficult to comprehend, and some forms of comprehension are not wholly reassuring precisely because of the strong sense of tedium that endless and seamless time may evoke.) Being finite, temporal units are also likely to involve scarcity relative to the wide potentiality of time-consuming wants and activities. Thus activities tend to be *concentrated* in time—for example, the working hours—and *segregated,* with different times for different activities. Individual roles or group activities have temporal dimensions, but boundaries may not be absolute so that temporally segregated actions are subject to invasion. Time thus becomes, along with space, a way of locating human behavior, a mode of fixing the action that is peculiarly appropriate to circumstances.[7] Since both time and space are finite, the aphoristic "time and place for everything" has a distinctly limited validity: "everything" would quickly surpass the boundaries that time and space impose.

Temporal Ordering

Time presents itself in human experience as a boundary condition, but also as a sequence. The hands of the clock move, calendar pages are torn off, birthdays are celebrated with growing regret, officers retire, and eras come to an end.

Short of major and sudden geophysical events, space principally acquires any dynamic qualities it may have by virtue of changes in social values, interests, and techniques. In other words, space is generally a passive condition of behavior, variable only as human behavior makes it so. Time, on the other hand, is intrinsically dynamic, and indeed the idea of dynamic (or static) is impossible without reference to conceptions of time.

Much of social behavior depends for its orderly qualities on common definitions, assumptions, and actions with regard to the location of events in time. Certain activities, for example, require simultaneous actions by a number of persons, or at least their presence at a particular time—the starting of a work shift at a factory, the departure of a fishing boat from a wharf or beach, or the calling of an association meeting to order. Thus one element of temporal ordering is *synchronization*. Other activities require that actions follow one another in a prescribed order; thus *sequence* is a part of the temporal order. For still other activities the frequency of events during a period of time is critical; thus *rate* also is one of the ways that time impinges on social behavior. For all of these elements of social coordination the term *timing* is useful, since it denotes precisely the critical importance of some temporal order, while leaving open the kind of requirement or the rigidity with which the activity in question is to be related to time as an inexorable variable. Although any of the dimensions of temporal ordering may be subject to some latitude, some tolerable degree of looseness or approximation, timing is an intrinsic quality of personal and collective behavior. If activities have no temporal order, they have no order at all.

Although the life span would appear to set the upper limit of time perspective for personal ordering of actions and events, provisions for children or testamentary trusts for favored persons or organizations may prolong an individual's partial control of his significant world. The transmission of knowledge and values to new generations as well as the transmission of biological heredity add other facets to human continuity.

The degree to which man is a creature of circumstance and has essentially no control of the temporal order of his life is itself highly variable. Clearly some discretion in timing is a major component of any objective meaning of freedom. Yet in this as in all other relations between individuals and the social order discretion must be under substantial constraints if social life is to avoid chaos, that is, if predictable and patterned interaction is to continue.

Organizational Time

Some organizations have pretentions to immortality, at least by comparison with the limited life spans of their transitory members. Yet no organization completely escapes the boundaries set by time as a finite and scarce resource. The limiting cases are those of the theoretically complete totalitarian community or state and the custodial organization (the military camp, prison, mental hospital, or residential school).[8] Even here, however, it is unlikely that custody and surveillance will be so complete that all of the time of all members will be organizationally available, and in any event the organization does not escape from the limits imposed by the length of temporal periods—the day, month, or year—or from the fact that the number of members over whose time it exercises control is far from infinite.

As the example of "total" organizations implies, the most convenient measure of organizational time resources is that of person-time units (the equivalent of "man-hours" in conventional business computations). In societies that afford a wide array of organizations, as all modern industrial societies do, the temporal resources of organized aggregates range sharply downward from custodial organizations and work organizations to minimal-participation associations. In nonliterate and even in agrarian societies the family and kinship structure may take on many of the qualities of totalitarianism, with little activity time being exempt from the pervasive influence of an encompassing kinship organization.

Wherever roles are played out in the context of different concrete groups, the scarcity of organizational time and the scarcity of individual time intersect, for the claims of groups on members are likely to be competitive and add to a total greater than the individual has at his disposal. In general, groups will attempt to increase their temporal inventories. (Although this statement is elliptical, since groups do not think or act, it is essentially accurate, since persons acting for collectivities will seek to further common goals.) Thus, for the individual member facing competing claims, temporal divison or allocation and temporal priorities or sequences become major (though not exhaustive) alternatives in his relations with organizations. The individual may, for example, allocate a finite amount of time to each activity, or he may recognize the superior claim of one group and do its duties first, leaving later and residual time for others.

Particularly in the largest and most complex social groups invented by man, the bureaucracy or administrative organization, temporal order is of the essence. Synchronization, sequence, and rate of activities operate within narrow tolerable limits. Moreover, present actions must be taken in order to assure the outcome of future events, often over a considerable period. If individuals may, in small ways, extend their temporal influence beyond their own lives, the bureaucracy may in some of its plans act as though the awkward fact of human mortality did not exist. Just as the leaders of nations commonly attempt to assure a benign or at least tolerable future for generations yet unborn, the executives of private business corporations may commit current resources to investments that cannot realize a return during the lifetime of any current employee.

The quest for a worldly immortality by individuals, corporations, or nations may add modestly to the finite supply of time, but it avoids neither its ultimate scarcity nor the complex and hazardous problems of maintaining a temporal order. Commuters still miss trains, executives still make untimely decisions, and nations still fall behind in international races for weapons or influence. A sense of current urgency, probably more acute and affecting more people than ever before in man's history, prompts a new regard for clocks, both real and figurative. For the measurement of time is at once a symbol of man's attempt to order and control time and a symbol of time's fateful final mastery over the human enterprise.

NOTES

1. A. N. Whitehead, *Science and the Modern World* (New York: Macmillan, 1931), p. 47.
2. Richard Schlegel, *Time and the Physical World* (East Lansing: Michigan State University Press, 1961), Chapter I, "Time and Physical Processes."
3. See, for example, *Cold Spring Harbor Symposia on Quantitative Biology*, Vol. 25, "Biological Clocks," 1960; also Curt P. Richter, "Biological Clocks in Medicine and Psychiatry: Shock-Phase Hypothesis," *Proc. Nat. Acad. Sci., USA*, 46, 1506–1528, November 1960; Frank A. Brown, Jr., "Living Clocks," *Science*, 130, 1535–1544, December 4, 1959.
4. See Pierre Lecompte du Noüy, *Biological Time* (New York: Macmillan, 1937).
5. See Michael A. Wallach and Leonard R. Green, "On Age and the Subjective Speed of Time," *J. Gerontol.*, 16, 71–74, January 1961. For a review of research on subjective time, see Melvin Wallace and Albert J. Robin, "Temporal Experience," *Psychol. Bull.*, 57, 213–236, May 1960.
6. See Pitirim A. Sorokin and Robert K. Merton, "Social Time: A Methodological and Functional Analysis," *Amer. J. Sociology*, 42, 615–629, March 1937; also, Sorokin, *Sociocultural Causality, Space, Time* (Durham: Duke University Press, 1943), pp. 171–215.
7. See Amos H. Hawley, *Human Ecology* (New York: Ronald Press, 1950), Chapter 15, "Temporal Aspects of Ecological Organization."
8. See Erving Goffman, *Asylums* (Gordon City: Doubleday Anchor, 1961); Gresham M. Sykes, *The Society of Captives* (Princeton: Princeton University Press, 1958).

II

Individual Time Patterns

Two

The Temporal Location of Activities

From birth to death the human individual never quite escapes from the limits of time and its fleeting quality. The temporal mechanisms of the infant impose a fairly rigid set of requirements on the environment if he is to survive. He can live only a few moments without oxygen and only a little longer without food and liquid. Being totally unable to sustain life unaided, the human infant in a sense imposes time demands on adults or older children who are responsible for his care. The molding of biological tensions—especially hunger, thirst, and fatigue—by the social constraints of "proper" times for taking nourishment and sleeping [1] is commonly one of the earliest phases of socializing the young, that is, securing their adaptation to the requirements of a social order.

The physiological time demands persist throughout life, even though partially modified and often greatly elaborated. Eating and elimination, waking and sleeping come to be hedged about by a great variety of conventions, but, if the organism survives, the body imposes limits on social ingenuity in rendering it into something nonbiological.

The supremacy of human physiology as the principal focus of action, almost complete with the infant, diminishes in the process of reaching maturity, so that the devotion of virtually all time and energy to simple survival is universally regarded as exceptional and in a fundamental sense "dehumanizing." Other demands appear and multiply: the demands of social performance in an unavoidably social species. These demands, too, have temporal implications that may be as arbitrary and peremptory as the need for air or food. It is the social being more than the biological organism that primarily concerns us here. Although in this and in Chapter 3 the static and dynamic aspects of time patterns are viewed as they bear on the individual, that individual is a social actor, a role player. The principal sources of constraint and order, of temporal differentiation and sequence are to be found in society and culture, built in part, it is true, on the biological foundations of the human organism.

The Constraints of Time

The distinction between time as a boundary condition and time as a flow of events, though somewhat arbitrary, is meaningful in the patterning of social action. If events were endlessly novel, not only would predictable order in life be impossible, but so too would notions of time itself.[2] It is the rhythmic recurrence of patterns that permits the sense of structure and the sense of temporal units. Recurrent sequences may determine the temporal units that form boundaries for action, and within those boundaries allocations must still be made. The day, for example, may be viewed either as a cycle of sequential activities (perhaps "one damned thing after another") or as the fixed boundary within which the demands of the body, the mind, and the social system must be satisfied by activities, each of which involves an allocation of time from a small finite supply. The principle of the boundary is not changed if the cycle is longer: the week, month, season, year, or even the lifetime. The ordering of activities is, of course, a major mode of allocation of temporal demands. To this our attention turns in

Chapter 3. Ordering also commonly involves marking off some kinds of units, and the limits imposed by these boundaries claim our attention now.

Variations in Temporal Perspectives

It might be supposed that the wider the boundaries of time perceived—that is, the longer the time perspectives or horizons—the less urgent or demanding the rigidity of minute temporal location. Yet this rarely appears to be the case. A short-term perspective may encourage either a fatalistic or a frivolous attitude toward the uses of time. The scriptural admonition, "Take no thought of the morrow; sufficient unto the day is the evil thereof," was based on the assumption of the imminent second coming of Christ and the end of the world as then constituted. On the other hand, a desperate effort to crowd into compressed time as much experience as possible is likely to emerge from an *unexpected* foreshortening of temporal horizons: the diagnosis of an illness as quickly fatal or the expectation of imminent disaster. A long-term perspective, we shall see, is commonly associated with precise identification of short segments.

*Time scarcity in some absolute sense may be greatest where man's relations with his environment are extremely insecure as the ordinary state of affairs. Thus many nonliterate or "primitive" groups have poorly developed techniques for providing sustenance and for the preservation of individual lives. Yet the uncertainty of life generally does not produce a careful fractionation of temporal units, a tidy husbanding of the "manifestly" short and precarious supply. Indeed, the complaint is often voiced by the Western observer—more often someone with interests in securing indigenous employees than the anthropological scholar attempting to analyze an alien culture—that primitive populations have "no conception of (or perhaps regard for) time."

The paradox becomes complete by contrast with the clock-ridden member of a modern industrial society. The inhabitant of one of the world's prosperous countries has an average life expectancy at birth of about seventy years,[3] and adults, having survived the hazards of childhood, can expect to live to a somewhat more advanced age.[4] Though the chances of premature death by disease or accident are by no means eliminated, such misfortunes are sufficiently rare to give virtually every person a "reasonable" expectation of a normal life span.

For the modern man, too, the exigencies of sheer survival are attenuated or removed entirely. A substantial portion of his waking hours is likely to be "discretionary" from the point of view of economic survival, though of course economic production is never an adequate description of societal needs. (Biological survival requires something approximating family functions for the procreation and rearing of the young, and social survival requires attention to social discipline and protection, maintenance of motivation and preservation of values, and, critically, a way of determining who does what.[5]) Even from a less economically restrictive or more socially adequate view of the demands of the environment, the denizen of an advanced society is likely to have more truly discretionary time—the true meaning of leisure—than his primitive or peasant counterpart. Yet the urgency with which the limits of time are perceived in industrial societies is immeasurably greater than in those social systems in which one would suppose time to be scarce and its limits narrowly circumscribed.

This paradox, that time is perceived as scarce in measure that it becomes relatively plentiful, requires explanation. The explanation lies in the combination of two other characteristics of the "advanced" civilization. (The quotation marks are inserted for the benefit of those who profess to doubt that the change from the simple life constitutes genuine progress.) Those characteristics are the extreme *specialization* of social roles and of the functions of social organizations and the introduction and spread of precise *measurement* of time based on an arbitrary extension of astronomical cycles.

Time scarcity, in an operational sense, is clearly increased with the multiplication of potential claims on the same temporal units. For the primitive food gatherer or cultivator the struggle for existence may be hampered by the shortage of time (that is, of inputs of activity), but the scarcity situation is more likely to be perceived, and usually correctly, as a shortage of resources, the failure of rain, or the adverse effects of insects or beasts. Additional labor inputs without technical improvements will not increase the supply of sustenance or its certainty. Although the producer is by no means immune to inconsistent demands—the interruption of work by a passage ritual such as a wedding or by a periodic festival—these demands are likely to fall at infrequent intervals. The modern man with memberships in many groups, often with membership as well as function specialized to a high degree, must play different roles with different people. The insistent expectations to which he is subject may be temporally ordered, but they are unlikely to be in any precise and unproblematic way.

Specialization leads both to temporal role conflicts, that is, competing claims for various activities with limited time precluding complete compliance with all demands, and to the competitive building of person-time inventories on the part of organizations that have different and preclusive membership. For example, an American voter may not recognize any role conflict in the appeals of Republicans and Democrats, but partisan success may be a function of political participation. For the politically active member of either party the threat of the adversary may well increase the salience of his own political commitment, to the potential detriment of other temporal demands. In this way organizational competition may have consequences for role competition even for the person who is not a member of the competing organizations.

Temporal measurement provides the mechanism for marking off precise units and thus tends to heighten the awareness of and the significance of finite boundaries. The expectation of a long life does not make death less certain; on the contrary. The value of time tends to be judged in terms of its use, and if measurement permits a more precise temporal ordering it does not effectively increase the total supply available for competing claims. Temporal precision may, it is true, make possible the segregation of roles, but in doing so it may also permit the multiplication of activities defined as different and thus result in a crowded or even hectic schedule, with the strains induced by temporal boundaries enhanced by strains induced by any errors in the schedule or its performance in action. The executive, for example, who divides his daily schedule into fifteen-minute units increases the probability that his use of time will entail tensions.

Time boundaries, then, tend to be vague and somewhat flexible when measurement of intervals and durations is not precise. The boundaries also tend to be vague when the specialization that prevails more nearly differentiates between persons than between various activities expected of the same person. The sociological concept of *role* involves performance according to expectations of a position (status) in a group or other context of social behavior. Except for purely titular or honorific statuses in which the role requirements are essentially nil, positions entail action and thus time allocations. The point of this conceptual clarification in the present context is that encompassing and therefore preclusive statuses are likely to be differentiated from one another according to their appropriate temporal patterns, but as such they have little bearing on temporal *constraints*. For example, age and sex are universal bases of social differentiation; in every case social definitions are elaborated from a physiological base and other expectations that are physiologically arbitrary are also likely to exist. It is only when the boundaries between these global statuses are vague—for example, the duties of youths and adults or men and women—that role strain and therefore time strain may occur. Note that for the social group the lack of status flexibility (for example, in an emergency) may introduce a major strain in maintaining continuity of function while protecting the individual from any uncertainty. The man who refuses to do a woman's work or vice versa may be on perfectly sound and absolutely mischievous ground.

It is only as global statuses are broken down into specific role demands in several different contexts that temporal boundaries become interesting. Without assuming that age and sex roles are uniformly free from internal strain, we may note that another biologically based status distinction clearly entails multiple roles.

This is position in a kinship structure. Thus the adult male may be "simultaneously" son of living parents, husband, father, nephew, uncle, and cousin. Depending on kinship practices, he may also have various significant affinal or "in-law" relations with his wife's kinsmen. He will always have some such role relationships, even if the role requirement is one of avoidance (which takes its own toll of time and energy). Now, from a structural point of view these statuses may be "simultaneous" and perhaps represented as such on a more or less elaborate kinship chart. From a behavioral point of view they are likely to require differential action and therefore temporal allocation. This is one principal reason for supposing that even if temporal allocation may not be precise in unspecialized societies some allocation is still necessary.

Beyond the cycle of waking and sleeping and the temporal demands implicit in multiple kinship roles, what kinds of temporal constraints occur in primitive societies? Weather and the seasons affect most human societies and may limit productive activity. The interruption of "normal" activities by rest or recreation appears uniformly but with varying periods. These cycles affect the distinction between work and recreation and have prominent elements of sequence. As such, they are discussed later, but they are interesting in the present context only because cycles entail boundaries. It is noteworthy that the periodic respite from regular activities is subject to alteration only in genuine emergencies, that is, in situations recognized as exceptional and critical. The mere fact of precarious sustenance, if "normal," does not produce unending productive effort. The indigenous Australians, though hunters and food gatherers and thus users of the simplest known economic technology and in constant danger of starvation, periodically interrupted work for recreation and ritual observances.[6] The "corroboree" has become synonymous with the moral holiday, an indulgence that believers in the primacy of materialistic motives find it hard to explain, much less to approve.

In many primitive societies specialization of functions is so small that in the daily routines it is difficult to distinguish work from nonwork, whether for persons—workers and "dependents" —or for temporal roles. Among all the socially useful, or at least socially sanctioned activities, which are to be taken as labor and which are not? [7] Nevertheless, Stanley Udy's comparative evidence rather indicates that some organizational differentiation is fairly common, particularly for tasks requiring unusual numbers or unusual skills.[8] These tasks, however, are rarely daily or, in that sense, routine. Being exceptional, their performance must impose some temporal constraints on routine performance.

When labor is not in short supply, in relation to land and the available technology, considerable filling in for those diverted to other activities may be possible without gross impairment of normal production, although clearly with some increased temporal constraints on those doing "extra" service. Thus in the subsistence or traditional sectors of the economies of sub-Saharan Africa the work of males absent as migratory wage laborers may, within limits, have slight effect on the output of food crops, for their wives, kinsmen, and co-villagers may do the necessary agricultural work. A gross shortage of young adult males will, however, reduce the land in cultivation or the necessary work during the growing season.[9]

The temporal constraints set by the typically short *average* life expectancies in nonindustrial societies are not exactly the obvious ones. First, the high mortality conditions that yield life expectancies at birth around thirty to thirty-five years [10] are likely to be highly selective by age and, in particular, to be especially severe for infants and children. Thus infant mortality during the first year of life, which may be at reported rates upward of one hundred per one thousand live births [11] and are probably higher, have an extremely depressive effect on averages. Put more positively, for adults who have survived the rigors of infancy and childhood mortality rates may not be grossly higher than those in more technologically advanced areas. Nevertheless, adult mortality is likely to be high enough to set underlying and perhaps even recognized limits on long-term temporal horizons. On this question there is little evidence. There is, however, a subtler point to be noted. Marion Levy has pointed out that with high mortality rates elaborate kinship systems are more likely to be ideal than actual for the simple reason that death will have left many nominal kinship positions empty.[12] The implication of this circumstantial argument is that kinship role requirements, if mandatory and not simply contingent on the availability of role players, will place additional duties and correlative temporal demands on "substitute" kinsmen. This problem is readily and nearly universally recognized as applicable to the widowed parent. The extended kinship system, typical of most nonliterate and agrarian societies, increases the likelihood of "absentees by reason of death."

Before turning to the temporal boundaries characteristic of various positions and roles in strictly modern societies, a note may be added concerning the boundaries of time as developed by the "regular" clergy in medieval monasteries. According to Lewis Mumford, the clock, though not precisely invented by the monks, was brought to a much higher state of precision and reliability by them.[13] As the religious orders were to live by rule (thus the "regular" clergy), the allocation of time for sleep, work, and devotions was regarded as of crucial importance. Thus, to the paradox that time is perceived as scarcest where in some ways it is most abundant, we may add the paradox that the fundamental machine of an industrial civilization was developed by persons of such unworldly religious orientations that they withdrew from ordinary mundane life. The bells of monasteries and churches, of course, came to have an impact on the temporal order of communities while reminding the faithful of the eternal order represented by religious regularity.

Competition for Time

In contemporary complex societies the role demands on individuals are manifold, and many of them derive from distinct groups or systems of action. For the preschool child the temporal limits of his activities are gradually modified from his physiological needs to the conventional patterns, not wholly arbitrary, imposed by his family. As he develops peer-group relations, the boundaries become more constrained, as physiological "needs" (for example, the midday nap) are subject to the alternative possibilities of play. Then to the family and peer group is added the school, which entails a rigorous temporal discipline for beginning and ending the school day and also for most activities in between. The school day tends to be marked off into precise segments, and segmental tasks are set despite the circumstance that learning speeds of children are likely to be rather different. School, for as long as the child persists in formal education, tends to have as peremptory a claim on blocks of time and often about as disciplined an allocation of time as the job has to the adult wage earner.

By the assignment of homework the school may extend its temporal control even beyond its physical boundaries and formally allotted hours, with consequent problems for the child and therefore for adults of temporal allocation among family, school, and play or peer-group activities. As the child grows older, he may be given a gradually increasing range of temporal latitude, of partial control over the order of actions, but within a system of more or less firm performance demands and disciplines. This broadening sphere of decision (and therefore uncertainty) presumably encourages preparation for adult roles but may well increase the stringency of ultimate temporal boundaries if the liberty accorded has been used unwisely or frivolously.

To adult work roles we shall return shortly, but nonworkers (that is, persons not directly recompensed for their activities) also operate under temporal constraints. Many of these constraints as they bear on the housewife and mother not only require adjustment of schedule to the externally fixed timetables of schools and employers but also the business hours of shops, the weekly cycle of work, recreation, religious participation, and activities of membership associations of one sort or another. The nonworking mother in an industrial society tends to be subject to the time disciplines of her husband's work, but also to be the arbiter of the out-of-school schedule of children and perhaps of the residual resources of time subject to family disposition.

For the formerly employed adult beyond retirement age, or the housewife with no more children in the household, the temporal boundaries are so loosened that time itself may acquire a negative value rather than operating as an all-too-scarce resource. But even as the day and the week may seem to take on the qualities of an excess of time, because duties are relaxed and temporal disciplines diminished, the proximity of death steadily advances. The aged, particularly in industrial societies,[14] may be caught in the highly ambiguous situation in which they have too much time for much too short a future. Unless victimized by really acute physical or psychic distress, aged persons are likely to cling to life tenaciously and thus to be very aware of life's final boundaries although currently bored with excessive time for the shorter units of the clock and calendar.

The Worker's Time

The worker in modern industrial societies, and particularly in the large-scale manufacturing establishments that help to determine their distinctive character, is subject to an extremely elaborate and detailed time discipline. Whereas most workers in most economies, historical and near-contemporary, have been primarily task-oriented, the great majority of economically active persons in industrial societies not only work on a rigidly determined time schedule but also are recompensed in terms of temporal units at assigned tasks; that is, they are paid for work by the hour, week, month, or year. For the primitive food gatherer or peasant cultivator time as such is not economically valued. He pursues a particular task or set of tasks steadily, except as he is interrupted by darkness or fatigue, until the work is completed, and then may spend a variable period "doing nothing" until the next endeavor is started. The factory or office worker may be held to minimum task-unit standards and may in fact be financially rewarded for exceeding some product-time standard, but not only is his workday and workweek fairly fixed but his temporal constraints and recompenses within those units are highly standardized. The transition from a temporally lax and variable work pattern to a tightly timed and temporally recompensed work schedule is one of the major changes in attitude required of the newly recruited worker in underdeveloped areas undergoing economic modernization.[15]

The timing problems—synchronization, sequence, and rate of actions—inherent in complex organizations of work can most appropriately be viewed from the standpoint of the administrative organization itself (Chapter 5). For the worker's role many of the organizational timing problems become simply the length and rigidity of the temporal units by which he is governed.

The Pace of Productive Activities

Owing once more to the combination of minute specialization and precise measurement, some industrial workers are held not just to daily or hourly time boundaries; minutes and even seconds may mark off one sequence from the next repetitive action. The work is endlessly repetitive, save as the clock gives surcease at the end of a day's labor. Semiskilled workers in operations involving sequential assembly, often depicted as "typical" industrial laborers, are outstanding examples of extremely fractionated time units of activity. With machine pacing the temporal restraints may be extreme, but some variations in rhythm, such as earning a brief respite by greater speed and "working up the line," may still occur.[16]

The workers not directly paced by the machine is still not exempt from short temporal rhythms. "Scientific management," or, more properly, time-and-motion studies, establishes by direct administrative authority what the machine does indirectly: a closely timed sequence of actions.[17] (Machines, of course, also represent instruments of administrative authority. As Feldman and Moore have commented, ". . . the men whose acts determine the machine are never the men whose acts are determind by it." [18])

Machine pacing does not end with the machine tender, for the men responsible for material supplies and product storage are fairly closely linked to the temporal demands of machine rate. However, even for these workers, the temporal units within which tasks are to be completed and then repeated in the next time period tend to be much longer—expressed in minutes or hours rather than seconds. For some workers, such as the monitors of instrument boards for largely automated processes, the required *attention* may be constant, though other duties are infrequent and, being of a "rectifying" variety, at variable and unpredictable intervals. Here the very lack of routine may give time a negative value.

The web of occupations related to physical production spreads far. Salesmen, though their own work schedules may be rather flexible but are tied to the schedules of those they call on, can set delivery dates on orders only by reference to present production schedules or to past schedules if the goods are to be drawn from inventory. Interdependence and coordination generally require simultaneous presence of workers and managers, clerical workers and staff advisers, internal communicators and external representatives. The workday, if not its internal fractionation, affects a considerable proportion of the employees of any establishment.

The questions of fractionation and temporal boundaries are not unimportant, however. Generally speaking, the wider the latitude in the order of tasks, the wider the latitude and variability in the fractional temporal restraints in the workday. The intermediate manager, for example, may be chiefly responsive to the communicative cues of others—often his superiors. Thus he first "clears the in-basket" of letters and memos before he has any discretionary (but still "official") time uses. The executive, though pressed upon from every direction, inside and outside the organization, has a job that positively requires initiative, and initiative is more the instigator of time demands than its recipient.

Work Schedules

Since some 85 per cent of the American labor force represent wage and salary earners,[19] the "workday" is an extremely common temporal unit. (The proportions of employees among the economically active, though variable in industrial societies, is always a majority and in totalitarian economies nominally includes all workers, including collective farm workers.) Even for such workers the workday is by no means standard across occupational lines and certainly not historically.

Since the early years of the first industrial revolution, when fifteen or sixteen hours a day were the standard for industrial operatives, the long-term trend has been downward to the seven- or eight-hour day.[20] (Much shorter workdays negotiated with employers in 1961 and 1962 in the United States by certain building-trades craft unions probably were designed primarily as surreptitious wage increases, as the difference between a con- tractual four- or five-hour day and a normal work period must be compensated at overtime pay rates.) The changes, however, have not been steady over the short run but are rather a set of sharply interrupted plateaus, with each reduction spreading rapidly across industrial and occupational lines and then usually holding steady for a number of years or even decades.

Both Georges Friedmann and Harold Wilensky,[21] in brief reviews of the historical evidence on the workday and workweek, emphasize that the industrial revolution initially *lengthened* the temporal demands on the productive worker. The twelve-hour day, with an hour or so off for eating, was common in Nineteenth Century English and American factories. Allen Clarke, in a de- scription of a Lancashire mill town,[22] noted that workers were warned of the impending day's toil by a steam mill whistle at 5 A.M. Lest this be insufficient alarm, "knockers up" went around rapping on bedroom windows with long poles.

Among the countervailing effects of subsequent mechanization have been the shortening of the workday and week, on the one hand, and the rigidly bounded temporal fractions governing routinized labor, on the other. In other words, tasks become more closely timed but for a shorter daily period.

The workday and workweek are usually linked in discussions of trends and differentials in the hours of labor. For many pur- poses this is sensible, since the week also comprises a conventional and relatively short temporal unit, and a long day may be offset by a short week and vice versa. However, as Wilensky has noted,[23] the two measures are somewhat independent and have rather markedly different implications for the pattern of leisure and other nonwork activities.

Although the industrial worker and other "bureaucratized" employees represent the "norm" for work patterns in industrial societies, other somewhat less clock-driven occupational types are worthy of comment. A task orientation of work has not been entirely eliminated. Some occupations provide somewhat flexible temporal limits without intricate temporal coordination with others—for example, free-lance artists and writers, researchers, scholars of many types, many salesmen, fund raisers, and piece-rate interviewers for polling organizations. Other persons have jobs based on irregular but not self-determined patterns. These are, in general, persons whose service involves problem solving for others, and problems have a way of being temporally undisciplined—for example, some physicians, lawyers, dentists, funeral directors, clergymen part of the time, firemen and some policemen, temporary office workers and substitute school teachers, maintenance and repair men, and consultants of various descriptions. Most professional entertainers may have highly disciplined work schedules, but at times complementary to ordinary working hours so that their work can provide a leisure activity for patrons. Whether the executive with his homework-laden attaché case is slow, ambitious, or exploited, his extra work invades his other time commitments or residual discretionary (leisure) time. Wilensky's sample of occupational types clearly indicates that at least some of these people with discretionary schedules (executives, professionals, and proprietors) work substantially longer days and weeks than those more closely disciplined by timetables of activities.[24]

The long work schedules of many who have considerable control over their time is only partly offset by a tendency to take longer voluntary vacations than those bureaucratically employed. Others (particularly farm workers and factory workers with modest education, skills, or employment seniority) may have "involuntary" vacations deriving from seasonal work, layoffs, or time lost in changing employers.[25]

The Working Life

Because of the lack of a clear distinction between working and not working in tribal and agrarian societies, comparison of the time demands (and limits) of work is not possible across such a broad spectrum. The same is true of the work life cycle, for the tendency in nonindustrial societies is to assign tasks of some sort to anyone with the physical capacity and dexterity necessary to do something useful. Children were also amply represented in the factories of the early Nineteenth Century. The combination of required public education and laws regulating minimum age for workers later increased the age of labor-force entry; that trend has continued, with the further extension of education and especially the increasing numbers completing secondary and even college and professional courses before their fulltime entry into work. Yet the trends in the United States during the present century are summarized by Wilensky: "Despite an increasing age of entry into the labor force and a decreasing age of exit, men today work more years over the life cycle then they did in 1920." [26] The main explanation of this anomaly is the substantially decreased likelihood of death during mature years, so that more men have a full work cycle and live to retire.

The boundaries set by the length of working life are somewhat less interesting than questions of sequence and careers. Yet certain boundary problems are significant. For example, the age-patterning of activities is crucially affected by the difference between a sharp break between work and retirement at a mandatory age (most frequently 65 in the United States) and a "gradual" reduction of activities or no retirement at all available to the moderately healthy oldster whose time dispositions remain his own to the end. At the beginning of work, also, the postponement of full labor-force participation by more and more advanced and specialized education clearly "shortens" the work life cycle, except that professional workers with such educational qualifications tend to be least subject to daily and weekly time disciplines (though actually working long and presumably hard) and are least likely to experience a sharp terminal boundary between work and retirement.

A Woman's Work Is Never Done

The duties of women in modern societies have some peculiar features with respect to temporal boundaries and locations. First, it must be noted that by conventional definition of the labor force housewives are excluded as not "gainfully" occupied, although their services could be given a market value and if not available would indeed require substitute employment. Second, for the normal adult female, familial obligations tend to have top priority even for the working wife, and this holds even where the female labor-force-participation rates are high, as in the Soviet Union. In the United States the highest labor-force-participation rates of women are for the ages 20 to 24, chiefly comprising women who are unmarried or married and childless, and for ages over 40, mainly women who have no young children in the household or no dependent children at all. The pattern of early childbearing and its early termination (most commonly before age 30) has resulted in a reservoir of "employable" time for wives whose families have entered what sociologists stickily but insistently call the "stage of the empty nest." [27]

The housewife, though not a "worker," does have tasks, many of which are temporally linked to the work schedules of men and the school schedules of children. It is generally conceded that the various "labor-saving" appliances, common to the American household and increasingly available to the households of Western Europe, have at the least reduced the physical drudgery of housework. It is also commonly assumed that labor-saving appliances are time saving,[28] but William Goode and Sebastian de Grazia enter sharp dissents,[29] noting that home machines, like those in factories, are time demanding both when they are operating and especially when they are not and require waiting for repairs.

One major housewifely activity involves consumer purchases.

The housewife's predominant control over "routine" expenditures —food and those clothes that are inexpensive or have a short life expectancy—is associated with other role characteristics, but time availability is certainly relevant. When wives are employed at hours approximating those of the husband, joint shopping appears to be the norm. The time spent in shopping may be considerable, even for food. The supermarket achieves its principal cost saving not in economies of scale but in increasing employee productivity by passing along the bulk of the labor—selection, assembly, and delivery—directly to the consumer. For many housewives, however, the time is not "wasted." Marketing becomes, once more, a social event comparable to primitive markets. By a temporal coordination, perhaps accidental in origin but deliberate in continuation, housewives meet to chat over traffic-blocking wheeled baskets of food.

Clearly the major labor-saving device benefiting the housewife in industrial societies is the contraceptive. It is chiefly the housewife without preschool children who participates in bridge groups, joins associations both frivolous and uplifting, and possibly attempts to advance her husband's career by judicious entertaining. She may even become a full-fledged, recompensed, and, therefore, counted worker, a labor-force participant, which indicates that one use of her somewhat discretionary time is to cast discretion to the winds and circumscribe her day by the dual disciplines of home and work.

Leisure: Residual and Discretionary

In industrial societies the trend of a century or more has been toward a general or average reduction of work time. Workdays and weeks have been shortened, clearly demarcated vacations have become the norm for both the employee and many of the self-employed, and the combination of greater longevity and standardized retirement ages have added greatly to the person-years of postretirement life (and, incidentally, a great expansion of research and writing on the problems of the aged). However, in a longer time perspective or over a wider cultural comparison the substantial amount of working time not spent at work by adults is by no means a peculiar phenomenon of contemporary affluence in the economically advanced countries. Wilensky cites historical sources regarding the large number of rest days, holidays, and other days marked off from "normal" pursuits in the Roman calendar [30] and summarizes his point by noting that the modern worker has achieved about the same amount of leisure as his counterpart in the Thirteenth Century.

Although annual "calendars" are generally not available for nonliterate societies, over the shorter term something like a "weekly" cycle is widespread. In some instances the "unusual" days are set aside for various recreational and communal activities. Inca law, for example, provided that three or four times a month all inhabitants of each village should feast together for "friendship, rejoicing, and relaxation." [31] In other societies the cycles may be longer—for example, a whole month of rest and feasting among the Annamites; [32] and in many societies, with or without a "weekly" cycle, feasts are "occasional," that is, they mark events such as births, marriages, and deaths.

In societies with a settled agriculture and some handicraft specialization the phenomenon of the periodic market is common.[33] Webster [34] generalizes that the length of such "weeks" tends to be related to the technological level, as economies with "primitive" technology also are likely to have "primitive" storage facilities. Such markets, as often noted,[35] are multifunctional; that is, they accomplish the economic functions of exchange while also serving as centers of communication, the occasion for courtship, and the locale for various forms of recreation.

Leisure: Not Working

But what is the meaning of leisure, and why is it widely thought to constitute a social problem? At least for modern economies that afford a clear-cut market test for activities that are labor and those that are not, leisure may be defined residually as waking hours not spent at work. By this definition, however, the largest "leisure classes" in order of magnitude would be children before entrance into the labor force, adult women of working ages (say 20 to 65) not in the labor market, and a major portion of persons older than 65. The idle rich and the involuntarily idle poor constitute a much smaller category. The balance of leisure time, so defined, would be attributable to the nonworking hours of the gainfully occupied population.

Such a "residual" definition of leisure yields a large man-hour total, but, when that total is divided among the categories of persons who share in it, it is clear that their situations are rather distinct. For children and women there are substantial time and role demands that are virtually as peremptory as those affecting the worker. School hours are fixed for the school population. Housewives may have greater latitude in the temporal ordering of their lives, but part of that ordering is fixed by the school hours of children and work hours of husbands. School children and housewives, like the workers, may experience time constraints, "too little time," in view of primary and residual time-consuming role demands. On the other hand, for aged persons who are not economically active and for institutional populations and the involuntarily unemployed the "residual" designation of leisure may be more accurate. The problem here, in general, is that of "too much time." [36] Thus for some distinct and rather populous segments of industrial societies the impression of hurry and bustle, of severe time restraints deriving from time measurement, time evaluation, and a plethora of competing claimants simply does not fit. The constraints of time, though still real in the long run, may be minimal on a daily or even annual basis.

The amount and disposition of the residual time of workers combine and accentuate the two questions: what is leisure and why is it a problem? Simple answers are to the effect that leisure is nonwork time, that it has grown by virtue of the reduction of working hours, and that it may not be used "constructively" either for the individual personality or for the social order. Yet the simplicity is deceptive and somewhat spurious, and the subject must be further pursued.

Residual nonwork time is by no means "free" or unconstrained.

As Bennett Berger writes, ". . . the very idea of free time belongs to a presociological age. If sociology has taught us anything it has taught us that no time is free of normative constraints. . . ." [37] Now Berger's final statement may be readily accepted but without the kind of deterministic overtone that his general discussion implies. This overtone derives from the circumstance that he is explicitly using a "functional-equilibrium" model of society, wherein all parts mesh and the individual may be viewed as a controlled mainfestation of the requirements of the system. If, however, the system itself displays tensions and strains, both in static cross section and as it moves through time, the constraints it exercises on individuals are by no means unitary and unambiguous. The "operational" meaning of freedom is choice, and, if the person is faced by genuinely competing alternative uses of his temporal resources, he must "decide" (or perhaps drift into a course of action). [38]

Leisure: Optional Use of Time

It is in this operational sense that leisure may be positively, rather than residually, defined as *discretionary time*. The principle that no human behavior is exempt from normative controls is perfectly consistent with some "freedom" in the choice of those activities that one will engage in and be bound by.

The extent of leisure so defined and the way in which truly discretionary time is used are only beginning to be intensively studied,[39] partly because the methodological problems of observation are fairly severe. Gross differentials in various "participation rates" by age, "class," and occupational category have been established,[40] but they necessarily miss the subtler question, the degree to which in some sense these residual-time activities are part of a "syndrome" appropriate to the social category in question and thus afford little discretion. This question may be seen in extreme perspective by the apparent contrast between the partly successful attempt at a carefully controlled and often mandatory use of nonwork time in the Soviet Union [41] and the wide options (including the option of apathetic withdrawal) available in pluralistic societies. In fact, the actual exercise of discretion in time use in a totalitarian society would be antisocial were the system "pure," for such discretion would impair the high degree of social and personal "integration" that such systems foster. There are strong indications that such is the official view of Soviet ideologues.[42]

Where many genuine options for use of time exist and the representatives of activities—ranging from promoters of commercial entertainment to promoters of worthy causes—press their claims on possible participants, differences in actual participation may be taken as a crude indicator of preference. (Without some intensity scale, of course, the indication must be approximate: for example, time spent at religious observances gives little evidence, one way or another, of religiosity.) Though De Grazia espouses the tendentious view that "true" leisure consists in thought and contemplation and is thus perforce limited to an élite few,[43] we are by no means constrained to accept his position, for it has no relation to his factual studies of activities in time.

Repeated studies have confirmed the correlation between class position and participation in various associations.[44] Even if the warning is heeded that the groups characteristic of lower economic sectors are simply less "formally" constituted and named —"the pub is the poor man's club"—it still appears that the participation of the poor has a higher probability of being relatively unorganized or passive.[45]

For many purposes of social analysis "class" is an extremely crude indicator of differences, and Wilensky has established firmly some of the underlying variables that account for observed class differences and make the sources of similarity and difference more precise and indeed less subject to class distinctions as such. Primarily, his research indicates that the "high participators" are those who have "stable careers."[46] Now, such careers show a substantial correlation with educational levels and, to a lesser degree, with income, but within a broad band of social class, even a "high" one, those with unstable careers behave about as apathetically as their somewhat more numerous counterparts in lower economic groups.

The Problem of Leisure

This evidence leads us back once more to the still unanswered question why leisure is regarded as a problem. If we leave aside juveniles, the aged, and the unemployed as those having "too much time," attention is focused precisely on the relation between work and leisure and particularly the possibility of substituting the satisfactions of leisure for the lack of satisfactions in routinized, socially sterilized, and essentially meaningless work. Many years ago I suggested [47] ". . . that the great recent concern about 'training for leisure' is largely an attempt to make out-of-work activities supply the creative activity that industrial work fails to provide." It is, in other words, *alienation* from work that turns the constructive critic's gaze to the hours out of work.[48]

Here we encounter another set of dilemmas and paradoxes. First, it is clear from Wilensky's data that the main beneficiaries of the "new leisure" in the labor force have been those who had the longest hours a century ago, namely, the "hourly rated" employees.[49] Yet the most prominent of the long-hour workers are those professionals, officials, and the like who have both the widest discretion in the length of their work time and the disposition of their time within those boundaries and who also turn up as the "high participators" in hobbies, associations, and other presumably constructive or creative activities.

Arnold Feldman and I have suggested a theoretical resolution of this paradox, which is given empirical support by the precision of Wilensky's identification of the occupational and career patterns of those who have a high social participation. (Such clear empirical confirmation of theoretical developments can by no means be taken for granted in the social sciences.) The solution suggested was a rejection of the hypothesis of frustration—say alienation from the job—compensated by diverted activity—say meaningful leisure activities. The alternative theory was offered, ". . . according to which both dissatisfactions and satisfactions are mutually reinforcing, and thus individuals' levels of participation and involvement are generalized rather than compensatory." [50] Nothing, we argued, fails like failure, just as nothing succeeds like success.

Leisure, then, is a problem where work is a problem, and probably proportionally. The "constructive" use of leisure is likely to depend in considerable measure on the constructive definition of jobs. This is a position emphatically espoused by Berger, who offers a "normative" definition of leisure that would not sharply distinguish between financially rewarded and other activities. By this view, ". . . leisure refers to those activities whose normative content renders them most important to us, those things that we want to do for their own sake or those things that we feel ethically (as distinguished from expediently) constrained to do." [51] This is consistent with the view that some occupations, at least, do not afford a clear distinction between work and leisure, as work is partly playful and leisure is partly creative.[52] Berger rejects this view, professing to find verbal expressions of "cynicism" about work even among professionals and thus a kind of universal alienation from work.[53] There is no evidence, however, that this "sophistication" runs so deep that commitment to callings is rare or absent altogether. Wilensky lends some inferential support to a "cynical" view by commenting on the apparent preference of the self-employed for more money rather than more leisure.[54] The direct evidence lends itself equally well to the interpretation that some workers genuinely like their work, and the undirect evidence of high social participation outside the job can otherwise scarcely be explained at all.

The boundaries and constraints of leisure time thus remain factually somewhat variable and theoretically somewhat fuzzy. The social scientists now asking much more precise questions than their predecessors and using some refinements in seeking answers may help in more exact location of activities not caught up by the great organizational patterns of work, school, and home.

The scarcity of time, though ultimately absolute, is also relative to the level of "demand" for its use. The picture that emerges from our survey of leisure is that the demand may be less than the current supply of time for those whose interests and aspirations have not been extensively enmeshed in the network of social life, whereas others feel the pressure of time precisely because there are always interesting ways of using it. Since dichotomies, including this one, are likely to be false, one might imagine a "perceived scarcity-scale of time." Such a scale might well be an extremely sensitive index of the degree of "integration" of persons into the rich fabric of a pluralistic social order. For our final paradox relating to temporal constraints is that it is only when the *scarcity* of time is a problem that its use is likely to be consistent with personal creativity and socially approved values.

NOTES

1. See Nathaniel Kleitman, *Sleep and Wakefulness* (Chicago: University of Chicago Press, 1939); also, Vilhelm Aubert and Harrison White, "Sleep: A Sociological Interpretation," *Acta Sociologica,* 4, 46–54 in Fasc. 2, and 1–16 in Fasc. 3, 1959 and 1960.

2. See Richard Schlegel, *Time and the Physical World* (East Lansing: Michigan State University Press, 1961), Chapter I, "Time and Physical Process."

3. See United Nations, *Demographic Yearbook,* 12th ed. (New York: United Nations, 1960), p. 119. The expectation of life at birth in industrialized countries ranges from about 64 to about 75 years, depending on the country and sex.

4. For example, in the United States, the life expectancy of a male at birth in 1958 was 66.4 years; at 10 it was 59.0 years; at 40, 31.1 years. *Ibid.*

5. See, for example, Marion J. Levy, Jr., *The Structure of Society* (Princeton: Princeton University Press, 1952), Chapter IV, "The Functional Requisites of Any Society."

6. See, for example, W. Lloyd Warner, *A Black Civilization* [New York: Harper, 1937; Sir Baldwin Spencer and F. J. Gillen, *The Arunta* (London: Macmillan, 1927)]; Geza Roheim, *The Eternal Ones of the Dream: A Psychoanalytic Interpretation of Australian Myth and Ritual* (New York: International Universities Press, 1945).

7. See Wilbert E. Moore, "The Exportability of the 'Labor Force' Concept," *Amer. Sociolog. Rev.,* 18, 68–72, February 1953.

8. Stanley H. Udy, Jr., *Organization of Work* (New Haven: HRAF Press, 1959).

9. See Wilbert E. Moore, "The Adaptation of African Labor Systems to Social Change," in Melville J. Herskovits and Mitchel Harwitz, eds., *Economic Transition in Africa* (Evanston: Northwestern University Press, in press—1963), Chapter 13.

10. For example, India (32.45), Greenland (32.17), and Guinea (30.5). *Demographic Yearbook*, pp. 602–609.

11. *Ibid.*, pp. 512–521.

12. See Marion J. Levy, Jr., *Some aspects of the Analysis of Family Structure* (mimeographed; to be published).

13. See Lewis Mumford, *Technics and Civilization* (New York: Harcourt, Brace, 1934), pp. 12–14. Mumford's views are supported in general by Sebastian de Grazia, *Of Time Work and Leisure* (New York: Twentieth Century Fund, 1962), pp. 41–45, 303–304. On the other hand, the discussion of the development of the clock presented by Lynn White, Jr., makes no reference to the role of monastic orders; see *Medieval Technology and Social Change* (Oxford: At the Clarendon Press, 1962), pp. 119–129.

14. See Wilbert E. Moore, *Industrial Relations and the Social Order*, rev. ed. (New York: Macmillan, 1951), Chapter XXI, "The Aged in Industrial Societies." See also Harold L. Wilensky, "The Uneven Distribution of Leisure: The Impact of Economic Growth on 'Free Time,'" *Social Problems*, 9, 32–56, Summer 1961, especially pp. 46–47; Michael Wallach and Leonard R. Green, "On Age and the Subjective Speed of Time," *J. Gerontol.*, 16, 71–74, January 1961.

   For a perceptive discussion of the differing temporal perspectives of various age categories and a positive view of constructive use of time by the aged see R. M. MacIver, *The Challenge of the Passing Years: My Encounter with Time* (New York: Trident Press, Simon and Shuster, 1962), especially Chapter VII, "The Changing Face of Time." MacIver also comments on the way that some units of time, such as a decade related to age (the 30's, 40's, or 50's) may not provide tight restraints because they are perceived as comprising an "indifferent interval," significant only as its terminus is approached. See his Chapter XII, "The Indifferent Interval and Other Protections."

15. See Arnold S. Feldman and Wilbert E. Moore, "The Work Place," in Moore and Feldman, eds., *Labor Commitment and Social Change in Developing Areas* (New York: Social Science Research Council, 1960), Chapter 2.

16. See Charles R. Walker and Robert H. Guest, *The Man on the Assembly Line* (Cambridge: Harvard University Press, 1952), especially p. 39. See also Walker, *Modern Technology and Civilization* (New York: McGraw-Hill, 1962), especially Part Two, C, "Revolution in the Machine-Man Relationship."

17. See, for example, Georges Friedmann, *The Anatomy of Work* (New York: Free Press of Glencoe, 1961).

18. Feldman and Moore, *op. cit.*, p. 19.

19. See the *Monthly Report on the Labor Force* (United States Department of Labor), May 1962. On that date the exact figure was 83.9 per cent.

20. See Wilensky, *op. cit.*
21. See Georges Friedmann, "Leisure and Technological Civilization," *Intern. Soc. Sci. J.*, 12, 509–521, 1960; Wilensky, *op. cit.*
22. Allen Clarke, *The Effects of the Factory System*, rev. ed. (London: Grant Richards, 1898).
23. Wilensky, *op. cit.*
24. *Ibid.*
25. *Ibid.*
26. *Ibid.*, p. 36.
27. On the "life cycle" of the family, see Paul C. Glick, *American Families* (New York: Wiley, 1957). See also Sidonie M. Greenberg and Hilda Sidney Krech, *The Many Lives of Modern Woman* (Garden City: Doubleday, 1952), especially Chapter 6, "The Empty Nest."
28. See Wilensky, *op. cit.*, p. 54.
29. William J. Goode, "Industrialization and Family Change," in Bert F. Hoselitz and Wilbert E. Moore, eds., *Industrialization and Society* (The Hague: Mouton, 1963); De Grazia, *op. cit.*, pp. 161–163, 397.

    For estimates of the time spent in housekeeping and child care, see James N. Morgan and others, *Income and Welfare in the United States* (New York: McGraw-Hill, 1962), Chapter 21, "Time: The Third Dimension of Welfare."
30. Wilensky, *op. cit.*
31. El Ynca Garciloso de la Vega, *The Royal Commentaries of the Yncas*, translated by Clements R. Markham (London: The Hasluyt Society, 1871), Part I, Vol. II, p. 33.
32. See Pierre Gourou, *Les Paysans du Delta Tonkinois: Étude de Géographie Humaine* (Paris: École Française d'Extrême-Orient, 1936), p. 408.
33. See Wilbert E. Moore, *Industrialization and Labor* (Ithaca: Cornell University Press, 1951), pp. 226–228.
34. Hutton Webster, *Rest Days* (New York: Macmillan, 1916), pp. 117–118.
35. See Sidney W. Mintz, "Peasant Markets," *Sci. Am.*, 203, 112–122, August 1960; also George Dalton, "Economic Theory and Primitive Society," *Amer. Anthropologist*, 63, 1–25, February 1961.
36. The literature on problems of the aged is tremendous. For the question of time dispositions one of the best sources is the collection of papers edited by Robert W. Kleemeier, *Aging and Leisure* (New York: Oxford University Press, 1961). On the leisure activities of the unemployed see Eli Ginzberg, *The Unemployed* (New York: Harper, 1943); E. Wight Bakke, *Citizens without Work* (New Haven: Yale University Press, 1940); Mirra Komarovsky, *The Unemployed Man and His Family* (New York: Dryden, 1940).
37. Bennett M. Berger, "The Sociology of Leisure: Some Suggestions," *Ind. Relations*, 1(2), 31–45, February 1962, quotation from p. 38.
38. This is consistent with the view espoused by Shackle. See G. L. S.

Shackle, *Decision, Order and Time* (Cambridge: Cambridge University Press, 1961).

39. See especially the various papers by Wilensky, references to which are included in his "Labor and Leisure: Intellectual Traditions," *Ind. Relations,* 1(2), 1–12, February 1962; also, De Grazia, *op. cit.*

40. *Ibid.*

41. Wilensky provides a brief summary in the article cited in Note 14.

42. *Ibid.*

43. De Grazia, *op. cit.*

44. See, for example, Mirra Komarovsky, "The Voluntary Associations of Urban Dwellers," *Amer. Sociolog. Rev.,* 11, 686–698, December 1946; Leonard Reissman, "Class, Leisure, and Social Participation," *Amer. Sociolog. Rev.,* 19, 76–84, February 1954.

45. See, for example, R. Clyde White, "Social Class Differences in the Use of Leisure," *Amer. J. Sociology,* 61, 145–150, September 1955.

46. Wilensky, "Orderly Careers and Social Participation: The Impact of Work History on Social Integration in the Middle Mass," *Amer. Sociolog. Rev.,* 26, 521–539, August 1961.

47. In the first edition of Wilbert E. Moore, *Industrial Relations and the Social Order* (New York: Macmillan, 1946), pp. 294–296, quotation from p. 295.

48. See, for example, Berger, *op. cit.* Friedmann, *op. cit.,* Chapter VII, "Leisure and Dissatisfaction with Work."

49. Wilensky, *op. cit.*

50. Feldman and Moore, *Labor Commitment . . . op. cit.* Chapter 4; quotation from p. 64.

51. Berger, *op. cit.,* p. 38.

52. See, for example, David Riesman, *Individualism Reconsidered* (Glencoe: Free Press, 1954), Chapter 13, "Some Observations on Changes in Leisure Attitudes."

53. Berger, *op. cit.*

54. Wilensky, *op. cit.*

    In their discussion of the contributions of time to family "welfare" James Morgan and his associates note that hours of work (including housework) and income are positively correlated over most of the income distribution, since leisure apparently is chosen as a substitute for additional goods and services only at upper income levels. See Morgan and others, *op. cit.*

Three

The Ordering of Individual Lives

Time in its passage is marked by events, most of which for most people most of the time fail to achieve the memorable significance of an Event. Recurrent activities tend to define the boundaries of temporal units of longer or shorter duration. The coincidence and sequence of distinct incidents provide the sense and reality of ordering events in time. Though life may not seem melodic to its participants, it is marked by rhythm and tempo and by chords and measures. The recurrence of temporal order permits predictability. Its total absence is psychologically intolerable. On the other hand, short-cycle repetition that is "endless"—permitting perfect predictability—is also intolerable, either for physiological reasons of fatigue or for psychological reasons of boredom. Uncertainty beyond some tolerance limit is likely to produce a breakdown in the capacity to act, often marked by apathetic withdrawal. Certainty to an insufferable degree may also produce rejection, hostility, or even occasionally such innovative changes as the deliberate introduction of risk. Since the upper and lower limits of temporal order are chiefly detected only by pathological behavior, the boundaries are likely to be variable by individuals and possibly by social groups or whole "cultures"; in any event, these limits have not been precisely determined. (The usual formulation for many aspects of human behavior, which begins "Beyond a certain point . . . ," should be interpreted as reading, "Beyond some point or area not clearly established. . . .")

The human infant, having few unlearned temporal patterns, must gradually acquire a complex set. Both synchronization and sequence are essential for manual manipulation, locomotion, and the gradual formation of coherent language. But the sequence of learning, too, is subject to restrictions of order. Some of these restrictions may be conventionally imposed—cultural convictions about the "right" sequence—rather than dictated by the physiology and psychology of "maturation." [1] The American mother who anxiously consults Arnold Gesell [2] to see if her child is hopefully advanced, disturbingly retarded, or just reassuringly normal is consulting a maturational timetable that may not have universal validity, as Gesell and Illg point out. Certainly the details must be different, for the things to be learned are not the same from one time and place to another. Beyond bare physiological necessities for survival and such universal physiological attributes of the human species as standing erect and walking, adult sexual intercourse, or the attributes of growing older, such as the onset of puberty and of female menstruation and the menopause, the temporal order is a social order. This complicates matters rather than simplifying them.

Timing Over the Short Term

As we move from the physiology of coordinated and sequential acts to interpersonal or social behavior, the proper timing of action becomes a matter of response to social rules, implemented by cues or symbols of some sort. Although simultaneous action by a plurality of persons requires a degree of social control that is by no means trivial, it is generally simpler in organization than sequential chains of action and certainly simpler than controlled rates of activity on the part of actors in a sequential and often invisible chain of specialization. Amos Hawley, writing about the "independent" community of food gatherers, comments, with dubious semantics, that, "Timing of activities is . . . principally a matter of synchronization rather than of coordination." [3] Yet the distinction is proper, if the term is unfortunate, for sequential temporal control is certainly more challenging than the securing of simultaneous and uniform response to a single signal.

Synchronization

The notion of synchronization is itself subject to close examination that is not entirely niggling. Since time is, in principle, infinitely subdivisible, being a continuum, just what is meant by doing things at the "same" time? It would be unduly cynical to say that the more accurate the measurement of time, the narrower the margins for deviation from simultaneity, yet precise measurements are likely to be put to some use and such uses have a way of carrying over into other activities. This carry-over is in some part the consequence of fitting social actions around the precisely timed ones—for example, the small temporal latitude allowed in the waking, dressing, and traveling time of the industrial worker who must report for work within a fairly narrow range of time, usually a latitude of less than ten minutes. In some part, also, the expectation of punctuality, where it is "required" for a complex and interdependent division of labor that is closely timed, may well carry over into activities in which synchronization is intrinsically less severe.

Synchronization without precise time measurement or an independent, aribtrary, and impersonal source (such as "standard time") is unlikely to be exact to the microsecond and is, in any case, dependent on response to a direct and common sensory stimulus. The audible signal (the horn or drum) may possibly give a prearranged signal for simultaneous action or may be used simply to summon members of a group to receive oral and visual signals. The use of direct sensory communication to secure synchronization and short-cycle rhythms is remarkably widespread and survives the invention of extremely accurate clocks. The cadence of hauling a fishnet to a boat or the shore, for moving a gigantic stone for building a pyramid, or pulling the oars of an ancient galley is matched by the bark of a military drill sergeant, the waving of a baton by an orchestral conductor, or the sharp demands of the coxswain of a racing shell. The fitting of melodies to synchronized cadences is a special, but by no means rare, illustration of the response to common sensory signals. It would be a brave man who maintained that the electronic assistance of the public address system which reaches beyond sight and human voice on the modern aircraft carrier with its peremptory and disembodied "Now hear this!" represents an untarnished improvement over the sea chanteys that paced synchronized movements on sailing ships.

Synchronization is perhaps most readily perceived where individual or undisciplined and intermittent effort is plainly inadequate for the accomplishment of some task. Thus work groups come first to mind. Yet close timing extends far in human relations. Eating together, for example, not only has certain utilitarian advantages for those charged with the preparation of meals, but also has universal significance as symbolizing "solidarity" or friendship and equality.[4] Physical or temporal segregation in eating always symbolizes some kind of social gradation and social distance. Thus separate, and postponed, eating by women in traditional Islamic and some Oriental societies is not a random social convention, any more than the refusal of White Southerners in the United States to eat "with" Negroes the food prepared by a Negro cook.

To give the signal for mealtime beyond the reach of eye or voice, an audible signal is common in societies with a "simple" technology, and the dinner bell is by no means unknown in suburban neighborhoods where wrist watches and radio transmission are available but needlessly expensive for the purpose at hand.

Perhaps the most frequent example of social synchronization other than eating is in sexual intercourse. From the general lack of discussion, or perhaps simply of information, one gets the impression that the achievement of simultaneous sexual climax is not problematical in primitive and agrarian societies. The impression may simply rest on ignorance, however. Sources of information on so intimate a subject may be difficult in cultures without marital counselors, gynecological physicians, and psychiatrists. The question may not have been asked in nonliterate societies on the shaky assumption of the psychologically untortured joys of simple savages. Certainly close synchronization is not automatic and "natural" for modern man, if the endless testimony of guides to marital happiness is to be taken seriously.[5]

Although modern industrial societies may be viewed as clock-ridden, the tolerable variation in punctuality is quite wide once one leaves the technological and organizational provinces of work and travel by public carrier. Unfortunately, there is no substantial research evidence on the norms and practices with regard to synchronization (or, for that matter, on most aspects of timing). One must go by casual reports and impressions. Meetings announced for a particular time may not be started then if an important official is absent or if, in a democratically organized association, a quorum of members is not present. As in many other aspects of social life, laxity in normative compliance is likely to become "perseverative," that is to become gradually more extreme until the trend is reversed by a kind of conservative reaction that reaffirms original standards. This "cycle of sin and penance," as it has been called,[6] may even be observed at the work place in situations in which the function of precise punctuality is more symbolic and administrative than required by intricate interdependence of action.

"Social" occasions, such as parties and entertaining guests at family dinners, also have a somewhat uncertain and variable requirement of punctuality. "Etiquette" books allow for substantial latitude for arrival at a cocktail party (for which the invitation often states a time range rather than simply a beginning time) but specify the importance of punctual arrival for dinner.[7] From casual observation it would appear that many people in the United States do not read, or heed, the etiquette books. The variation in practice is so wide that persons who are punctual may be referred to as "compulsive" about time, as though their conduct were faintly pathological. The norm of punctuality for guests appears to be stricter in Britain than in the United States, and probably also in Germany and the Low Countries, but less strict in "Latin" cultures.

Differences in temporal precision and latitude still abound in the contemporary world. The "voices of time," as Edward Hall calls the cultural assumptions about the temporal order,[8] are multiple and often discordant. The lack of clear norms commonly followed is productive of some tension in temporal co-ordination. The tension is fairly severe where cultural differences in time perspective and temporal value are concerned—for example, the standard exasperation of Anglo-Americans with Latin-American lack of punctuality and the absence of any apparent "error factor" in the tardiness to be expected.

Temporal Sequences

The sequential ordering of activities essentially provides a priority schedule in the strict sense, which may reflect priorities in the loose sense of relative values. Thus the admonition, "work before play," provides a rank order as well as a temporal order of actions. Similarly, in Christian tradition Sunday, the day of worship as well as of rest, is regarded as the first day of the week, though the secular view makes of the day part of the "weekend." Some Christian denominations require fasting before the religious sacrament of communion, thus giving a more precise temporal priority to religious observance. In such observances, but also in other ceremonial, judicial, and parliamentary organization, a strict order of procedure generally serves the practical function of proceeding by a predictable schedule and the rather more symbolic function of compliance with traditions, which always tend to surround recurrent matters of moment. Some of the efficacy of any ritual would be threatened by leaving out a portion or changing the order, even if these alterations were supportable on such practical grounds as hastening the procedure to completion.

Many games are organized so that they follow a more or less elaborate sequence, although within that sequence optional strategies, as in chess, may be the major element in determining the outcome. The alternation of offensive and defensive play in base-ball in a succession of innings, and with an established order of batters, or the alternation of moves in checkers and chess provides a temporal order with loose if any temporal constraints.

Conventional ordering, of course, also applies within temporal units. Housewives, for example, are likely to have a "normal" daily routine, modified perhaps by such weekly routines as wash-ing on Monday, shopping on Thursday, and housecleaning on Saturday. Although these sequences may be somewhat optional, the housewife is unlikely to be totally insensitive to the patterns set by her neighbors or to the variation in the supply and variety of food in the markets. The dietary schedule of Roman Catholics and Episcopalians may determine that if she buys fresh fish at all it must be on Thursday or Friday.

Somewhat longer temporal units such as the annual cycle of seasons require appropriately timed sequential actions so that, for example, crops are planted late enough to avoid frosts or the rot-ting of seeds in cold, wet ground but early enough so that they can come to maturity during the growing season. Conventional "rules of thumb" are likely to develop with regard to seasonal timing. These often use various "botanical clocks," such as plant-ing seeds when the leaves of particular trees reach a certain size in the spring. There are even longer time horizons: for example, the several-year cycle in one of the most "primitive" systems of agriculture, that of "shifting cultivation," which involves clearing and burning and repeating the process when soil fertility has leached away. In view of this extended cycle, the following char-acterization of indigenous African agriculture seems poetic non-sense:

Work . . . is dictated by the rhythm of the seasons . . . and all activities developed into a tradition sanctified by usage and surrounded by ritual. . . . Work in the tribal setting requires neither foresight nor planning; it includes no notion of time, there is no specialization and no order other than that ordained by the seasons.[9]

Norms of sequence apply to such seemingly ordinary activities as interpersonal communication and may become rather complex and correspondingly subject to error or failure in larger and more formal communicative networks. Perhaps the simplest forms of communication are the question and answer, the summons and response, the exchange of greetings. But who initiates the communication and the degree of requiredness in reciprocation may also be governed by norms. The rule that children should not speak until spoken to (commonly honored in its breach in American households) gives communicative priority to adults. In conversational and discussion groups in which participants are nominally equal the priority of speaking may have a high correlation with the informal status of participants, and high-status communicators may be accorded deferential silence and freedom from interruption that others cannot expect. Although the expression "speaking out of turn" often is a euphemism for saying the wrong thing, it may also be meant literally. Failure to respond to a communication is likely to be regarded as discourteous or as downright menacing, as when an employee's request for a higher salary is met with utter silence.[10] "The adage that 'no news is good news' is clearly a brave but vain attempt to suppress the mounting conviction that all is not well." [11]

The Rate of Actions

The temporal order that operates with flexible time constraints or only those imposed by the necessity, sooner or later, of doing other things may be compared to the task orientation of the primitive or agrarian producer. The tennis match, the rubber of bridge, the golf game are completed by accomplishment of a partly predetermined succession of events and not by the passage of time as such. When an order of events must be fitted into a more or less precise time period, the temporal order must include an activity rate. This is the common situation in industrial work. Variations in such activity rates may increase or decrease the actions that can be completed within a time period, but rates are also subject to the imposition of order whenever interdependent action is intrinsic to the action system. Before mechanical dishwashers, coordinating the rate of the washer and dryer of dishes provided a standard kind of temporal problem, trivial perhaps in the family kitchen and possibly important in the restaurant or institutional kitchen. Action that is "too fast" or "too slow" will upset the other elements of temporal ordering: synchronization and sequence.

In situations that allow some flexibility in temporal limits and rates knowledge and practice may be important determinants of activities per unit of time or in the accumulation of discretionary time. Thus in some, though not many, production jobs in industry unit-quota standards may be more stringent than uniform rates, so that the worker twice as proficient as the norm has more "rest" time or may actually leave for home when he has done his stint. The housewife who thoroughly familiarizes herself with the location of goods in a supermarket grocery may have more time to gossip while shopping or more time for other activities.

The desperate quest for speed, which some critics would regard as an endemic pathology of modern societies, may be interpreted either as an attempt to crowd more and more events into overly tight schedules or, in view of the hazards of accident or physical collapse, as a subconscious introduction of risk into an otherwise routinized round of activities.

The disciplined rate of standardized actions is certainly best exemplified in the organization of industrial production, but, to repeat, any combination of set time periods and set tasks necessarily has implications for the speed to be followed. The necessity is simply accentuated if different persons must be coordinated in sequence, as is typical of many industrial operations.

Communication exhibits problems in rate as well as in simple sequence. Almost instantaneous telecommunications provide a major change in the significance of space but do not "erase" it. The fixing of the diurnal cycle by the earth's rotation and the adoption of standard time zones result in another paradox, namely, that simultaneous communication or other activity may be far from synchronized. The time is simply not the same in different places.

The speed of communications has, in fact, many implications for strategies. One of the main impulses in this technology has been the competitive advantage of speed for economic, political, or military actions. Yet it is not uniformly advantageous. The "fast talker" is commonly distrusted as either a knave or fool. The response that is "too fast" raises doubts about the serious consideration given, just as the response that is "too slow" raises doubts about "reception"—has the intended recipient actually understood the message and how will he react to it?

Temporal Strategies

No social action is immune to normative constraints, which are usually expressed in the form of expectations of significant others. Yet the very precision of temporal measurement, the elaborate specialization of temporal duties, and the orderly arrangements for synchronization, sequence, and rate may give to the individual the negative power of mischievous disruption and some positive power of temporal strategies. The fine synchronization and precisely paced sequences characteristic of rationalized industrial production put a considerable power of disruption in the hands of any unit in an elaborately timed machine. Tardiness may delay the start of the whole system, and, theoretically, each part is so indispensable that the absentee would make operation impossible. The overly conscientious worker who does too much or works too fast may be at least as disruptive as the one who works too slowly, either because of incompetence or because he seeks to exercise a measure of control over the complex system.

Fighting the "system" is not the only way of using temporal strategies. We have noted that whenever speeds are optional or can be improved by knowledge and practice increased speed at set tasks can achieve discretionary time. If time and task are subject to close administrative control, subtler strategies may develop. When it becomes known that "efficiency experts" of one sort or another are attempting to set a standard for production units per unit of time, the pace may be deliberately slowed in order to hold some strategic discretionary pacing in reserve.

Laxity in temporal ordering permits a gamut of strategies. The "entrance" at a social gathering timed for greatest notice,[12] the deliberately late arrival of an essential member for a meeting, the carefully contrived telephone call to summon one away from a prospectively boring affair—these and many other tactics testify to human ingenuity in evading discipline or using it to best advantage. A whole exotic cult has been developed by secretaries in the fine art of maneuvering their opposite numbers into getting one principal on the line to be kept waiting while the other is told that the call is in order. The status symbolism of time scarcity may be far more valuable than any more practical uses and may justify long planning for brief successes.

The assumed value of time is, in fact, often unequal for various participants in social situations. The late-arriving official in our earlier illustration with regard to synchronization may be forgiven if his time is assumed to be more valuable than that of those who wait. Some colleges, for example, have more or less unofficially standardized periods that students are to await a tardy teacher, and in some instances the period is graded according to the teacher's rank. In all administrative organizations the differing values of time are likely to reflect formal rank rather precisely, yet the norm of punctuality inhibits the extensive "abuse" of status symbolization in American and West European usage. Patient waiting in the anterooms of officials is common and expected in many areas of the world.[13]

Competitive situations are the natural locales for development of strategies, some of which have important temporal dimensions. Since some measure of ignorance, including a lack of perfect predictability of outcomes, is an essential element in any enduring competitive system,[14] competitive strategies can be effective only if they entail some uncertainty or surprise. Thus in the "theory of games" rational play requires randomization of conduct over the short run—that is, the avoidance of clear and predictable sequences of action.[15] "Playing the clock" is an essential component of strategy in all timed games or in those that operate with ultimate time restraints. The competitor who is ahead attempts to slow down the pace of action, the prospective loser to speed it up. Temporal strategies in races may go so far as the entrance of a defensive contestant, whose mission is not to win the race but to set an impossibly fast early pace and prematurely wear out opponents so that a team-mate, following his own temporal strategy, may come from behind and win.

Such grand strategies have their homely and noncompetitive counterparts. The preparation of a dinner with a synchronized outcome or narrowly timed set of sequences requires knowledge of preparation and cooking times and therefore a *timed* sequence of activities in order to arrive at a synchronized result. If the culture's conventions condone and the family's affluence affords a diversified diet, each meal becomes a kind of freshly constructed timetable that can be made to sound as complicated as the mounting of a military maneuver.

Life-Cycle Ordering

For many persons the restraints imposed by the life span are less significant than its latitude in temporal ordering. Of course, the perception and significance of ultimate mortality is likely to increase with advancing age, with the prospective time remaining becoming increasingly precious. Bereavement also calls at least temporary attention to the reality of death, particularly if the deceased died "prematurely." It is reasonable to suppose, although there is little direct evidence on this point, that the time-constraining importance of death for, say, the young adult has an approximate correlation with mortality risks. That is to say, if killing diseases and frequent disasters are "normal" or if deaths in battle are numerous in military operations, those remaining alive may operate with rather short temporal horizons. In modern societies with low mortality rates, particularly for young and "mature" adults, those adults are likely to figure largely in the "many" for whom long-term temporal ordering is the predominant orientation to the life span. It is in these societies also that "infancy" is prolonged, in the sense of protracted formal educational preparation for future adult roles, and that intergenerational social mobility and some latitude in occupational choice provide precisely the options and uncertainties that permit and indeed almost require a kind of latitude in temporal ordering and potential strategies in sequence and timing.

Age Grading

Age, like sex, is a biological characteristic of the human species that no society can disregard. In both cases, however, the physiological phenomena set limits on social definitions of position and role but never adequately account for the actual cultural definitions and practices. The wide variations in age grading in human societies testify both to the ubiquity of age statuses and to the diversity of their number and significance.

Some peculiar problems of timing arise with regard to age and may be explored as a preliminary to the consideration of life-cycle ordering. The first problem is what is to be understood by the notion of an "age group" or the notion that persons are of "the same" age. Age clearly relates to the event of birth, and the measurement of age will thus hinge on the precision with which "calendar" dates and "clock" times are determined and recorded or remembered. Thus are persons of the "same" age those born in the same year, season, "sign of the zodiac," month, day, hour, minute, or, perhaps microsecond? One recalls the amusing opening passage in Laurence Sterne's classic *Tristram Shandy* in which the hero calculates the time of his conception to the minute, since (one is led to infer) the sexual act was interrupted by his mother's reminder to his father to wind the clock.[16] Tristram Shandy, like true believers in astrology to this day, professed his conviction that his fate was largely fixed by the time of his conception, though his reasons had more to do with prenatal environment than with the mysterious influence of the stars.

The fixing of what constitutes a common age is widely variable in practice, and extreme precision may be used to establish an age ordering rather than an age category—for example, the way seniority in grade is used in the United States military services or the assumption among Tibetan Buddhists that only one child is born at the moment of the Dalai Lama's death and inherits his spirit.

If an age group is thought to consist of those of the "same" age, then presumably the entire group moves simultaneously into the next older category. On the other hand, if the group is regarded as comprising a "band" of ages, older and younger still make a critical difference by the simple fact that the membership of the group will change as some reach the point of "graduation" (or superannuation) and others attain the minimum age for inclusion. Although ethnologists are often silent on this point, despite the extensive reporting on age grading, it appears that the age group is by no means so clear in its boundaries as often implied and that its age-based solidarity does not extend to a membership that is constant except for erosion by mortality.

A second problem derives from the first pair regarding age groups. It is the possible applicability of the concept of "synchronization" within life-cycle stages. If age categories are used as the basis of common role definitions within the category (of course, not all need be common so long as some are) and differential role expectations apply between categories, then the common patterns may be viewed as age-synchronized. This conception, however, is faintly tarnished if the category does not retain a relatively constant membership; at the least, the synchronization is likely to be more extensive for those of the "same" age than for a more inclusive age category. The question is likely to be partly factual —the actual precision of age measurement and the actual extent of age differentiation—and partly one of analytical convenience— the extent to which a problem of description and generalization requires the use of fine or broad categories. For example, one may generalize about "youth culture" or "teen-age culture" in metropolitan centers within industrial societies or seek out the subtype of eighteen-year-olds who have dropped out of secondary school.

The school, in fact, offers excellent examples of the way in which age and age groups intersect. If formal education begins for all children except a few "abnormal" ones at age six, as determined by the nearest birthday, and the curriculum is graded only by age, then the common educational demands for a school grade may be regarded as an example of synchronization. On the other hand, the elementary school, the junior high school, and the high school comprise students of several grades and ages. For those role prescriptions that are common to the whole category time in a sense stands still for the duration of a normal passage. This, of course, is simply another way of saying that age, being a manifestation of time itself, is a continuous variable, which may be marked off into more or less aribtrary and distinct units. Within those units time has distinctly static qualities, but the passage between units is intrinsically changeful.

The lack of age synchronization where in some sense it is expected is likely to be productive of strains. The school child who is far advanced or retarded for his age may fit awkwardly or not at all into the age-graded activities of classmates outside the classroom.

A far more extensive, and deeply institutionalized, strain arises from the lack of age synchronization in marital unions. This is typical of all Western societies, and in some, such as France, it is fairly extreme. Hence the ideal of the monogamous union, the pair marriage "for life," is impaired by a great excess of widows compared with widowers. Actually, this excess derives from three sources, one demographic and two sociological. First, although life spans of individuals are rather widely variable, averages are not. These averages in industrial societies indicate that women outlive men by upward of three years. Second, widows are less likely to remarry than widowers, the latter being more likely to choose much younger women who have not been married before. The widow, particularly if she has minor children, is generally not regarded as a good prospect. Finally, the life-expectancy difference is accentuated by the preponderance of marriages in which the wife is younger—on the average by eighteen months to two years in the United States. The synchronization of the duration of marital unions would be increased by marriages between spouses of the "same" absolute age, but even so women would be younger in what we might call relative or "actuarial" age. Thus women seeking to minimize the risk of widowhood or abbreviate its prospective duration would be well advised to marry younger men. As this solution is extremely unlikely, the strain is likely to persist. Clearly, this lack of life-cycle synchronization is one of the principal bases for the attempted reduction of the intrinsic strain by "insuring" the life of the husband and thus alleviating at least part of the penalty suffered by women as a consequence of their manifest biological superiority evidenced by their longevity.

The "age cohort," defined as those of the "same" age, has a special significance whenever there is substantial change in the social environment itself, independent of the mere fact of age progression.[17] (The type and rapidity of environmental change, along with such practical matters as the availability of information on age distributions, determine the suitable boundaries of age cohorts. In principle, the more rapid the change, the narrower the boundaries of those regarded as being of the "same" age should be.) The main point here is that in a society that is apparently changing only slightly during a normal life span, a society that is in a sense without current history, the succession of age roles may be regarded as a mere cyclical replication of the behavior of previous generations. If, on the other hand, the environment itself is changing, each age cohort has in a sense a unique history, for the intersection of novel events and particular ages is neither repetitive of the experience of previous cohorts nor a model for those that follow.

The significance of the age cohort is commonly expressed in popular literature by the vague and unsatisfactory concept of the "generation"—for example, the "disillusioned" or "jazz" generation of the 1920's or the "beat" generation of the 1950's. Generation is essentially a lineage term, the tracing of descent from common ancestors. As a temporal measurement, generation means the period between childbirth and parental procreation—the average around thirty years. Since children are being born "constantly," there is no such thing in a whole population as a common generation that can be assigned to a historic period. By inference from most of the discussion of generations, however, what is generally meant is an approximate age cohort around, say, ages 18 to 25. If made more explicit, and also preferably narrower and more precise in definition, the generational notion remains a useful one.

In its more precise form of the age cohort the conception of an age group moving through its own version of history has applicability not only to entire societies but also to more restricted populations, such as those entering particular occupations or even particular companies or other administrative organizations.[18] Just as the graduating class of an educational institution may have some continuing common characteristics (even if not reinforced by periodic "alumni reunions") despite their differing subsequent experiences, the entering class of recruits to managerial positions in a large corporation will if they continue with the same employer sustain an age-impact of significant events that will differ from that of their seniors and their juniors.

Age groups with common role requirements and common experiences may, we have argued, be thought of as synchronized. The underlying dynamic quality of age sooner or later asserts itself, however, and a prominent part of the life cycle is a sequential order of age-specific social positions and roles. The number and duration of significant age units are highly variable but generally include at least four or five—for example, infancy, childhood, adulthood, and old age. The transition from one category to another may or may not be sharp. If it is, it is also likely to be formally recognized and marked by a public ritual—a *rite de passage*, or passage ritual, as this class of ceremonies is technically identified.[19] In tribal and agrarian societies the transition from childhood to adulthood is especially likely to be clearly identified, and the failure of a clear transition (or, perhaps better, an unsynchronized succession of partial transitions) has been noted as contributing to the ambiguous position of youths in American and some other Western societies.[20]

Significant age categories of less than a year are fairly rare. The birthday and the end of a school year mark off annual segments, but some years are still more significant than others, such as the completion of one multiyear segment of education or the passage from one age category to another. (In a sense the school year's segmental terms and even shorter time units involve micrograding by age, but they do not seem to be socially defined as such.) Though the passage of years brings death closer, it may also bring rewards meanwhile. This is perhaps most clearly seen in achieving legal age and in the varieties of privileges and immunities that accrue with seniority (organizational age). The biological longevity of marital partners and the social longevity of their union may also be honored, conventionally in the United States at five-year intervals beginning with twenty-five duration-years.

It should also be noted in passing that the length-of-residence requirements for various legal and social benefits ranging from divorce (private relief) to financial assistance (public relief) give passage of time a positive value. These requirements produce their own strains in societies marked by intense residential mobility. Tax collectors, for example, seem more willing to assure newcomers that they belong than do tax dispensers.

If age has its privileges, which may be inconsistent with other bases for determining merit, they are not extensive in industrial societies. The "accent on youth" is genuine and general and derives primarily from the greater accommodation of youth to rapid social change and, indeed, the greater probability that innovations will be made and implemented by the young. Rules of tenure and other privileges of security may favor the older worker or citizen, but the onset of formal retirement may be regarded as a mixed blessing by those involved.

Age, being basically an exact function of time, should move at a steady rate. Yet "physiological age" or "social maturity" may differ from chronological age and from one person of the "same" age to another. Thus a person may be flattered as "mature beyond his years" or degraded as "old before his time." Aside from these variations, the relation of events to time requires the concept of rate to refer to the fast, normal, or slow pace at which individuals experience events as they get older. To the degree that latitude and differentiation in age performance are narrow, and optional age careers rare, one may reasonably think of persons moving through life's events at a standard, and unproblematical, rate. The degree of such standardization in traditional societies has probably been exaggerated, but it is certainly greater than the highly specialized and rapidly changing "mix" of adult roles in modern societies.

Ages and Careers

The school, we have noted, provides a detailed set of age grades but with competitive differentiation at each level. The differentiation at each higher grade becomes increasingly selective for the type of education that is provided and for its possible duration. Those receiving college and postgraduate education delay their entry into the labor force beyond the statistical norm but generally enter at a higher income and prestige level or move up faster and further. The advantage is likely to be enduring and perhaps even cumulative.

The increasing bureaucratization of the labor force means that the careers of a growing proportion of workers may be marked by one or even several critical age-grade relationships. The individual may be "too young" or "too old" for higher positions despite other qualifications. The relative ages of superiors and subordinates may affect the chances of the subordinates for advancement. The watchful waiting for the death or retirement of an aging executive is not a completely pretty picture nor does it gain value by rarity.

Career strategies may involve exceptional effort—that is, speed or the intense use of time—in order to achieve a certain position by a certain age and thus ensure or increase the probability of further promotions thereafter. The man who has fallen behind, who is "overage for rank," is likely either to be "frozen" in his position—time standing still, again—or even required to resign or retire prematurely.

The importance of an age cohort's unique history appears once more in careers. The college graduates of the middle 1950's, for example, were the survivors of small Depression crops of babies and by that numerical fact faced a much more auspicious competitive situation than the one that will face the graduates of the late 1960's, the vanguard of the "baby boom." Thus advancement rates relative to age were certainly more rapid for the earlier group than can reasonably be expected by those now in high school or college.

In other respects also the age rate of advancement may be affected by factors additional to the simple notion of merits in a competitive system. The notion of a "labor market," for example, is an abstraction of little meaning for the fates of those working because there is a different market for each occupation or group of closely related and somewhat interchangeable skills. The man wise or lucky enough to be in a rapidly expanding field may progress rapidly, whereas his counterpart in another occupation who is equally or better qualified by all objective tests of selection and training may grow steadily older but not much richer or more honored by rank and responsibility. Even if men are employed by the same administrative organization, which encourages a steady advancement with age (presumably because of the cumulative value of experience), the market shortage of the skills of one and the surplus of those of another will almost certainly affect the rate of their advancement. In colleges and universities the fact that mathematicians on the average reach the top academic rank several or many years younger than do their colleagues in classical studies may support the notion, comforting to mathematicians, that they are brighter, but it is surely affected by the shortage of mathematicians and the surplus of classicists.

The discussion of graded careers is applicable to less than half of the American labor force, according to Wilensky's data.[21] For many others their mobility marks no real advancement, and for some it may actually mean retrogression.[22] For those who remain essentially stationary, occupational events within the period of their working lives, perhaps nearly fifty years, may be essentially unrelated to age as such. Entering employment as youths and leaving as old men may be the only significant life-cycle landmarks in their lives as economic producers. For workers without highly trained skills for which there is an enduring demand, age is likely to have negative consequences for their continuity in employment or for their level of earnings. Unless fully or partially protected by seniority provisions, the older worker may be subject to increasing risks of unemployment, either because his age is a "real" handicap to the jobs for which he has had training or experience or because it is thought to be by employers, with the same result. The problem of workers technologically displaced intersects with time in another way also, namely, the training time to acquire another set of skills for new employment, the acquisition of a marketable talent to replace an obsolete one. It is training time, in fact, that reduces the occupational mobility of professional workers and makes an absurdity of the notion of the "universal expert." Life is simply not long enough to learn more than a fraction of what there is to know.

Career Strategies

Training time is one of the major obstacles to maneuverability or flexibility in career strategies. In fact, although the sheer temporal length of the life cycle would appear to provide maximum latitude in altering the sequence and speed of events, timing is still of critical importance, and early errors or misfortunes may be difficult or impossible to rectify later. The youngster who drops out of high school or is unable or unwilling to attend college may never be able to repair the disadvantage to his subsequent "life chances." Even when people have options and are not simply the creatures of inexorable fate, they may not have the wisdom or foresight to choose those options that would be most favorable over the ensuing years.

There are, of course, relatively short-term strategies in the "management" of one's life. Awareness of increasing age may spur individuals to attempt to alter the pace of events or at least of personal achievements. Comparisons with age peers are common, with depressing or exhilarating results, for in a competitive system age synchronization is not an automatic virtue. Simply to be "on the pace" is only to comply with an average, which is "normal" but not outstanding. The imminence of retirement (with the usually unspoken aftermath of impending death) may prompt some people to exceptional efforts in order to get a better match between expectations and achievements.

Rational strategies of life-cycle management include the maintenance of physical vigor and the prolongation of life by preventive and therapeutic medicine. Parents may plan the number and spacing of children in terms of some calculus of future financial costs and schedule their current savings to meet those costs, since hoped-for income increases are likely at best to be somewhat off-phase for future family needs.

Rational economic management involves attempts to cushion against short-term income losses by savings or disability insurance, to compensate for income reduction or loss in retirement by prior purchase of annuities, and to provide financial support for dependents by life insurance on the breadwinner. Life-insurance protection can be secured by a wide variety of policy forms ranging from basic term or temporary protection to policies that combine a substantial element of savings with the protection. Examples of the latter are endowment and retirement-income policies. The typical and popular form of permanent whole-life insurance uses a premium based on the mortality experience of large populations. Obviously at the older ages of issue the typical premium is higher because the mortality rate is greater or, put another way, the period of life expectancy is shorter. Obviously, the family of the insured who dies early in the duration of his policy receives proceeds much in excess of the premiums paid, whereas the insured who lives well beyond his expectancy may in fact pay premiums in excess of the face amount of his policy. Since permanent forms of life insurance include cash and paid-up values, however, there is considerable flexibility available to the insured as his needs for family protection decrease and as he himself plans for the period of reduction or cessation of his personal earnings. In this curious world one way to win is to suffer the ultimate loss, that is, by premature death.

The very possibility of temporal strategies involving life and death symbolize a degree of mastery over fate, but that mastery is still only partial, since death is inevitable. Indeed, rational action is of distinct but limited utility, for the planning of time's uses, the calculus of future costs and benefits, provides no answer to the ultimate meaning of life and death. For the rational and civilized man shares the same inexorable destiny with the improvident wastrel or the untutored tribesman. Perhaps in death they are all united.

NOTES

1. For a good discussion of the relationships among the psychology of "maturation," the nature of the subject matter, and the sequence of learning, see Jerome S. Bruner, *The Process of Education* (Cambridge: Harvard University Press, 1960), Chapter 3, "Readiness for Learning."
2. See Arnold Gesell and Francis L. Illg, *Infant and Child in the Culture of Today* (New York: Harper, 1943); Gesell and Illg, *The Child from Five to Ten* (New York: Harper, 1946); Gesell and Illg, *Youth: The Years from Ten to Sixteen* (New York: Harper, 1956).
3. Amos H. Hawley, *Human Ecology* (New York: Ronald Press, 1950), p. 300.
4. See *From Max Weber: Essays in Sociology*, translated and edited by Hans Gerth and C. Wright Mills (New York: Oxford University Press, 1946), pp. 402, 407.
5. See, for example, F. Alexander Magoun, *Love and Marriage* (New York: Harper, 1948), pp. 217–219; Walter R. Stokes, *Modern Pattern for Marriage* (New York: Rinehart, 1948), pp. 58–62.
6. Wilbert E. Moore, *The Conduct of the Corporation* (New York: Random House, 1962), pp. 199–201.
7. See, for example, Emily Post, *Etiquette* (New York: Funk and Wagnalls, 1955), p. 363, "The Curious Fault of Lateness"; also, Amy Vanderbilt, *Amy Vanderbilt's Complete Book of Etiquette*, pp. 261–262, 269–270, and 304, where she deals with the problem of "late stayers" rather than "late comers." See also Edward T. Hall, *The Silent Language* (Garden City, Doubleday, 1959), Chapter 9, "Time Talks: American Accents," especially pp. 183–185.
8. Edward T. Hall, *Ibid.*, Chapter One, "The Voices of Time"; see also Chapter Nine, "Time Talks: American Accents."
9. International Labour Office, *African Labour Survey* (Geneva: 1958), p. 140. For a discussion of the connection between types of economy and temporal concepts, see Hubert Griggs Alexander, *Time as Dimension and History* (Albuquerque: University of New Mexico Press, 1945), pp. 23–26.
10. See Moore, *op. cit.*, p. 67.
11. *Ibid.*

12. Parkinson provides some amusing rules for timing arrival and departure from cocktail parties. See C. Northcote Parkinson, *Parkinson's Law* (Boston: Houghton Mifflin, 1962), Chapter 7.
13. See Hall, *op. cit.*
14. See Wilbert E. Moore and Melvin M. Tumin, "Some Social Functions of Ignorance," *Amer. Sociolog. Rev.*, **14**, 787–795, December 1949.
15. See John von Neumann and Oskar Morgenstern, *Theory of Games and Economic Behavior*, 3rd ed. (Princeton: Princeton University Press, 1953), p. 146.
16. Laurence Sterne, *The Life and Opinions of Tristram Shandy, Gentleman* (Oxford: Basil Blackwell, 1926), Vol. I, Chapters I–V. (First published in 1759.)
17. See Norman B. Ryder, "The Structure and Tempo of Current Fertility," in National Bureau of Economic Research, *Demographic and Economic Change in Developed Countries* (Princeton: Princeton University Press, 1960).
18. See Ryder, "The Cohort as a Concept in the Theory of Social Change," paper presented at the American Sociological Association meeting, September 1959.
19. See Arnold van Gennep, *Les Rites de Passage* (Paris: Emile Nouvy, 1909).
20. See, for example, James H. Bossard, *Parent and Child* (Philadelphia: University of Pennsylvania Press, 1953), Chapter XIV, "Rites of Passage," especially pp. 289–292.
21. Harold L. Wilensky, "Orderly Careers and Social Participation: The Impact of Work History on Social Integration in the Middle Mass," *Amer. Sociolog. Rev.*, **26**, 521–539, August 1961.
22. See Harold L. Wilensky and H. Edwards, "The Skidder: Ideological Adjustments of Downward Mobile Workers," *Amer. Sociolog. Rev.*, **24**, 215–231, April 1959.

III

Temporal Structuring
of Organizations

III

Four

The Family

The human infant is not born into a society or nation or culture but into a family. If his birth is illegitimate or, for some other reason, a normal family unit is lacking, his physical survival and social acceptance depend on some substitute agency. The attempts to make such substitutes official and general, to disestablish the family as the main source of childbearing and childrearing, have been rare and generally short-lived. Since the family may be regarded as the primordial social structure in the social evolution of the human species, the fact that it is the first group for almost every member of the species means that each generation in a sense recapitulates that evolution. Of course, it does not follow that the child's successive encounters with other social organizations—a sequence that is markedly variable in time and space— has any necessary relation to the evolutionary sequences in the specialization of social organizations.

The family then is the first and virtually preclusive claimant on time in the human life cycle. The degree and form in which the family retains some primacy comprise the principal variables in its inventory of "organizational time."

The Family as Residual Claimant

In the comparative materials on human societies the family and broader kinship systems stand out as universal features of social organization and as the predominant structure in many nonliterate groups. In fact, the predominance of kinship organization in "primitive" societies is such that the family would appear to be the microcosm, since functions ranging from economic production to religious observances, from education to political rule are carried out by the same encompassing organization.

Though the family in many societies may indeed have far-ranging functions, its totalitarian character is bound to be less than complete because of another universal feature—the "incest taboo." All known human societies normally proscribe sexual unions and marriage between closely related kinsmen. Thus all known societies comprise a plurality of families and lineages, and their social organization must include at least the relations among these units. These relations include the rules of marriage and indeed a number of other rules and procedures: the allocation of rights in scarce values (property), the preservation of order (government), and quite probably the provision for collective protection. Even if in these interfamilial affairs individuals always "represent" their familes, and this cannot be taken for granted, the family as an organized unit, as a group of interacting individuals, does not have complete claim on the time of at least some members. (The modern breadwinner is in some sense representing his family, but to say that he is only playing a family role is not very useful and indeed misleading.) Once the theoretical obfuscation of treating kinship systems as totalitarian is recognized, it then appears that nonliterate societies indeed afford numerous examples of multiple-family play and recreational groups, work groups, war parties, political councils, and communal religious observances.

Specialization of Social Functions

This small tour into the exotic realm of anthropological discourse has been necessary to establish some kind of comparative basis for the family in urban-industrial communities. One other comparison may be noted. The American, Canadian, or Australian frontier family was in many cases relatively isolated and for considerable periods relatively self-sufficient. In these cases, however, not only were the families part of a larger organized society, but they took with them to their new outposts both the material goods and the cultural features of that society and rejoined it as rapidly as settlement and improved transportation made possible. The family in industrial societies has clearly "lost" many functions and activities to other agencies, and thus has lost time claims on its members, but the magnitude of the change should not be exaggerated by comparisons with a mythical past or contrast with somewhat imaginary alternatives in "simpler" societies.

The "loss" of family functions derives from structural specialization around separable social functions. This specialization, in turn, is related to the size of organized entities (economies, politics, societies) and to such technological elements as transportation and communication. Given these conditions, various social functions may be carried out by distinct organizations: the state, the shop or factory, the church, and the school. To a degree, then, the potentially encompassing functions of the family are reduced by the participation of its members, either individually or collectively, in structures that are superfamilial in membership and normally outside the household in location.

Structural specialization, however, is of two major varieties, and their significance for family time inventories is quite distinct. One type of specialization is that characterized by the differentiation of organizations which make distinct but possibly competing claims on the time and energy of individual members of participants: the family and the employing organization, the church and the country club, the political party and the adult school. This is the type of specialization usually discussed with regard to "role sets" and "role conflicts," and this is the type of specialization that is usually meant by the loss of family functions. These groups compete with the family, since participation tends to be individual rather than familial, and in any event the activities are organized in a way relatively independent of familial structure.

A second type of specialization involves persons, not roles. In other words, certain kinds of organizations or activities have virtually preclusive members of participants: belonging to one bars membership in others. The outstanding example is that of occupational specialization or "division of labor." The individual worker rarely has more than one occupation or employer. His specialized occupational role or category makes him eligible for or requires his membership in some associations but thereby bars him from others. (Where the individual in fact has more than one job or occupational affiliation, the role strain is comparable to that of complementary specialization, but it is likely to be more accute both because other roles are more severely constrained and because of the probable inconsistency in the various attributes associated with the normally distinct and singular statuses.) It follows that occupational competition, for example, is not of the same order as the competition between familial and occupational duties, for the former does not involve contesting claims on the scarce resources of a common member but rather the quest for relative position and privilege in a larger system of status and rewards.

The significance of preclusive specialization for the time dispositions of families is that it adds a differentiating dimension to that of complementary specialization. Thus the impact of the job, the school, or the church on the family will vary according to the particular type of activity the affected individual is engaged in. One may contrast the time dispositions of the sailor or traveling salesman with that of the free-lance writer who works at home, the boarding school with the day school, and the church in a sectarian community with the urban religious congregation. Some occupational roles are so extensive that they not only pre-

clude others of the same category but also virtually all others—
for example, the celibate priest and especially the member of a
monastic order, the organizer for a radical political movement,
and the custodian of inmates in a "total institution." [1]

The family, then, will have to share its members (other than
infants) with other organizations, and the particular demands of
certain types of mutually exclusive organizations will affect various families differently. Some of the differences will be further
variables by age and sex, familial role—differing educational demands on children and youths, and differing occupational demands on adult breadwinners.

The loss of family functions is most evident in the extension—
both in number and duration—of education in schools and in the
removal of most of economic production from the home so that
the link of the family to the productive system is in the specialized role of the breadwinner. Both of these trends are easily exaggerated and misinterpreted. Much of the educational development represents a major change in the magnitude of educational
activity and is not simply a transfer from family to school. The
absence of children from the family unit for large periods of
time is, of course, associated with the changing economic position
of the family. Yet the family has not lost all productive functions.
It is a major supplier of services consumed by the producing unit:
notably child care, cooking, laundry, housecleaning, and shopping by the housewife but including also a substantial amount of
home repairs. (It appears that home repairs and improvements
represent an example—there are many—of a partial return to
preindustrial social patterns following a period of sharp discontinuity with traditional structures.) If one adds that the family
rather than the individual is the normal consuming unit of the
economy, with market principles of distribution based on ability
to pay mostly ending at the household door, then bald allegations
to the effect that the family has lost its economic functions in
urban-industrial social systems turn out to be simply silly.[2]

Aside from the family's provision of most of its full-scale members with eating and sleeping facilities, and at least some facilities
for rest and recreation, it is well to recall its universal functions

that have not been substantially eroded by the claims and alternatives deriving from other specialized structures: sanctioned adult sexuality, legitimate procreation and physical sustenance of infants, and the placement of the infants in the wider social system (including especially their initial cognitive training and moral socialization). All families to some degree, and the nuclear (two-generational) family of modern societies to a high and almost exclusive degree, provide for sanctioned interpersonal affection openly displayed. In a society generally characterized by impersonal and often transitory relations the family as a social unit whose members are treated as something like whole persons, complete with emotions, performs a psychological (and therefore social) function of no mean importance.

Family Time Inventories

It remains true that the time inventories of most urban families in industrial societies are smaller than is typical in primitive and agrarian societies, although they may well be larger than they were, say, fifty years ago. The reduction of the work week and the partial school day rather than the "total" work day for youths have added at least discretionary time, potentially available for familial or at least home-centered activity, though the increase in the housewife's discretionary time may release her from the household and thus partly offset the other potential time increments. In the use of discretionary time the technological provision of home entertainment (for example, radios, records, and television) has certainly improved the family's bargaining position with respect to competing leisure activities.

For mature adults (aged 24 to 49) Sebastian de Grazia's data [3] on activities during a seventeen-hour day (6 A.M. to 11 P.M.) show that men spend a surprising eight hours (nearly half their waking time) at home on the average day—slightly more than 7 hours Monday through Friday, nearly nine on Saturday and more than eleven on Sunday. Women of the same age category less surprisingly spend nearly thirteen hours at home on the average day, with little difference between weekdays and weekends. Older members of families (50 and over) naturally include those who are retired and a disproportionate number of those who are physically restricted; older men spend somewhat more than two hours a day more at home than their younger counterparts and older women slightly more than one hour more than younger women. Comparable time budgets for children and youths are not available, but it may be supposed that for those under twenty there may well be a fairly high and consistent *negative* correlation between age and time spent at home. Naturally, the range of experience is affected by school calendars, by work and marriage among older youths, and by family life styles for all ages—for example, the working mother's infant child cared for at a day nursery at one extreme and the well-to-do youth who mainly entertains his age peers in his home at the other.

Many household duties are not highly specialized in terms of personal qualities or skills, so that person-time units may be somewhat more additive and interchangeable than in, say, complex administrative organizations. Thus the family's static temporal dimensions, its time inventory, may provide for considerable internal flexibility. The unemployed husband of a working wife may do the cooking and housework, and older children may provide at least part of the care of their younger siblings. Nevertheless, age and sex roles are given cultural as well as merely biological specifications, so that some transfers of duties are regarded as distinctly abnormal and others may be unthinkable.

The family is normally the sole claimant on the infant's time, which, however, is essentially useless. For others, the family is a residual claimant on the time of its members who have various extrafamilial obligations. It is essentially the wife and mother who not only prominently represents that residue in her own time dispositions but also tends to assert familial claims on discretionary time and to assign and rearrange the use of the current temporal inventory. The decisional power of husbands is certainly variable between families, ethnic groups, "classes," and societies, but the very temporal commitments of wives within the family tend to give them considerable authority in allocating and directing the time of others.

The family can less than ever be represented as a microcosm of

the great world, but at least that small and partial world tends still to be a female domain.

The Order of Family Activities

Individual time allotments to the family may add usable time to group-centered actions or simply add discretionary, unused time to some kind of activity within the physical bounds of the home. The function of the family in providing the place for "spending" leisure time is not trivial, nor is the amount of time so spent— around four to five hours a day for mature adults according to De Grazia's sample survey.[4] Yet what De Grazia's materials do not show, and what is most interesting from the point of view of the family as a collectivity, is the time spent in coordinated and synchronized activity. The distributive and aggregative time allotments to the family are clearly considerable and that part devoted to familial tasks is certainly consequential, yet the symbolism and reality of unity surely depend in part on genuine collective activity.

Family Synchronization

Eating together, it was noted earlier, has both practical and symbolic meaning. Feeding the children separately has the same dual meaning, although it is often rationalized solely on the practical grounds of keeping them to a schedule different from that of the late-arriving father. Family recreational excursions on weekends and vacations and family visits to relatives give token of unity, of doing things "together." (The "togetherness" slogan, avidly put forward by *McCall's* magazine for commercial purposes, has much of the guilt-ridden and slightly desperate appeal of the commercialized sentimentality of Mother's Day. Both represent a kind of quest for "Paradise Lost" and both rest on the idealization of a past that did not exist.) Yet families do commonly get together fairly regularly, often daily for the evening meal, at least when the youngest child is, say, 8 or 9 years old, and may synchronize behavior with a more extended kinship system on traditional "family" holidays. Since a multilineal kinship system makes the relatives of husband and wife equally important in principle, and to a large extent in practice, and these persons are not otherwise related, rules tend to develop for deciding which relatives will be seen—in other words, some kind of preferential priority (for example, for reasons of distance) or alternating sequence is established.

The symbolism of collective activity is important, and the occasions for such activity are also occasions for maximum pressure to secure group conformity. With the substantial social separation of mature generations intrinsic to industrial societies, the gradual or sharply delineated independence of youth becomes apparent as it does not join in collective family activities. For the young, the family "loses functions" to the peer group, and the synchronization of family activities is sharply curtailed. Parents are likely to try to postpone and minimize this evidence of partial dissolution of the family. On the other hand, in households with one or more aged parents of one of the spouses—the designation "doubling up" indicates the extent to which generational separation has been institutionalized—the oldsters may well desire to participate in collective family activities, to the distress of other members.

Since the modern family is a residual claimant on time, synchronization may be adversely affected by its lack in the schedules of outside organizations. Thus the father who works nights or week ends may have little waking time at home that coincides with the out-of-school hours of his children. He may in fact exhibit various physiological and psychological disorders because of his "abnormal" schedule.[5] Although the children of well-to-do families may be sent to boarding schools and summer camps, for most families a common vacation is the norm and its time will be located within the summer vacation months of school children. Attempts to "stagger" work schedules and school schedules in order to give fixed capital equipment more even use, and perhaps in the former case also to reduce some problems of traffic congestion on weekdays, would impair the common residual time available to the family unit. In some instances the lack of temporal coordination is anachronistic. French school children have a midweek holiday and attend classes on Saturday. As long as their fathers were on a six-day work week, the school week and the work week were at least "on phase." Now, for the growing number of fathers with two-day week ends the school schedule prevents Saturday recreational activities for the family as a whole or the two-day trip in the newly acquired family car.

Sequential Ordering in the Family

Although family units in industrial societies are typically separated by the maturity of children and broken by the death of one spouse of advanced years, the time horizons may still be multigenerational and in any event are long enough to present problems of long-term allocations and sequences.

Given a "full" life expectancy and an enduring union, the amount of time that a family includes immature children is dependent not only on the number of children but also on their timing and spacing. The contemporary tendency for early, frequent, but limited childbearing increases the likelihood that parents will spend many years together subsequent to the maturity of the youngest child. Paul Glick's study of the American family, based mainly on census data and vital statistics, indicates that about a third of the period of a normal marriage may be spent subsequent to the maturity of the youngest child.[6]

The concentration of childbearing before the mother's thirtieth birthday also leads to a shortening of the average length of generations and thus to some "speed up" of the long-term rate of population growth. More significantly for present purposes the shorter generations mean more youthful parents and thus some slight reduction in the different perspectives on morals and conventions that arise from the unique history of various age groups. The relative youthfulness of "complete" families—those with immature children—may also encourage common family recreation and thus slightly reduce the intrinsically divisive qualities of the diverse interests of the young and old.

The timing of children presents some interesting problems with respect to the rate and sequence of "asset" accumulation. If, as Gary Becker suggests,[7] children can be regarded as "consumer durables" (with rising repair costs through time), one may ask how they are interspersed with other family purchases. Although the evidence is flimsy, it appears that a major factor in the "baby boom" following World War II has been an alteration in priorities, temporal and otherwise, of children with respect to various consumer durables. Early childbearing, although reducing the time that the young married couple may lead an unfettered social life or even "get to know each other" (which is not necessarily accomplished before marriage despite the "romantic" basis of mate selection), may extend the time during which the older married couple may increase their purchases of both things and experiences after their financial responsibilities for children are fulfilled. However, in the study of two-child families by Charles Westoff and others early completion of childbearing was given by a small minority of respondents as a reason for a short interval before a third child.[8] Nevertheless, whether or not the family cycle is carefully calculated in decisions on childbearing, the pattern of early starting and early stopping of "accumulating" children is clear. Incidentally, the rapid rise of the use of baby-sitters over the last two decades is no doubt related to the increased residential separation of adult generations and the virtual disappearance of domestic servants from the middle-income household; it probably also indicates a greater tendency for young parents to engage in social activities outside the home and on an adult rather than total-family basis.

Phasing of Family Cycles

For families with the expectation of a relatively steady income each child naturally adds to the family financial burdens, but timing as such is of small consequence. For the growing proportion of families with the reasonable expectation of a rising level of income during the normal working life of the breadwinner early and closely spaced childbearing is almost certain to be "premature" or off-phase; that is, the rate of income advancement is quite unlikely to keep pace with the rate of family increase. Certainly the breadwinner's peak earning power is quite unlikely to occur before the wife's age of 30, when childbearing tends to end, and in fact is more likely to occur after children have reached maturity. Thus for the self-employed businessman, the professional, or the person in an administrative career a "completely coordinated" phasing of family build up and career progress would entail extended but infrequent childbearing by his wife and in fact might well extend beyond the wife's childbearing ability at menopause (from 40 to 45).

This problem of phasing is accentuated by the institutionalized separation of the generations, with the assumption that each young married couple will be "on their own" financially. However, the extent to which adult generations are in fact socially separated probably has been exaggerated by sociologists too much impressed with the functional importance of intergenerational mobility in industrial societies and too little concerned with study of the actual operation of the contemporary kinship system. The time spent visiting relatives or the frequency of telephone calls among them is not known, but these indicators of the extension of persistent familial ties between generations and among adult siblings would certainly be numerically substantial and hardly to be interpreted as simply anachronistic. Indeed, their frequency is probably increasing. Also, the persistence of property inheritance, which violates one set of norms relating to the "detached" nuclear family, is a major component of the maintenance of a multigenerational family system and an extended time horizon.

Property inheritance also tends to be off-phase for the financial needs of young parents. With the combination of early termination of childbearing—so that parents may be no more than 50 years old when their youngest child is married—and the extension of life expectancies, property may well be inherited when it is no longer of critical use: when the breadwinner of the second generation is approaching the peak of his own earnings and he no longer has dependent children. Again firm evidence is virtually nonexistent, but it appears reasonable to suggest that directly or indirectly it may be the grandparental rather than the parental generation that alleviates the financial burdens of the young married couple in middle and higher income groups.

All this assumes, of course, that decedents leave some sort of estate for their heirs, but this is certainly true of a majority of family lines if account is taken of the large and rapidly growing number of life-insurance policy holders. (The notable longevity of aged widows may delay and perhaps destroy actual intergenerational transfers. By rates prevailing in 1950 the median age of American wives at the death of their husbands was only 61 years, but their own age at death was 77 years, or sixteen years later.[9])

The legal and institutional developments with respect to intergenerational obligations have become rather asymmetrical. Although the duties of parents to children have remained strong or even extended, as in the case of lengthened education to be discussed shortly, the obligation of mature children toward indigent parents seems to have diminished. Private pension plans, social-security legislation, and even direct relief are accorded the aged, and in most states of the United States the ability of children to aid in support is treated as irrelevant. The duties toward parents governed by the mores rather than the laws appear uncertain and ambiguous, with perhaps a majority view that help should be accorded if urgently needed and without serious sacrifice to one's "own" family and that separate residence for the aged should be maintained if at all feasible. Children thus become extremely dubious "old-age-security" investments; if they were to be regarded only from the economic point, they would represent a luxury expenditure, not an investment.

The strategy of life-insurance purchases also presents some critical problems of temporal ordering. The maximum need for income protection for the breadwinner's dependents is at a time when he can least afford it, namely, when he is well below his peak income and when his young widow's income-earning capacity would be inhibited or impaired by the necessity of caring for dependent children. Unless the young parents receive intergenerational financial aid, their wise course in timing appears to be the purchase of low-cost term insurance, on which at the ages of early maturity they have advantageous premium rates because of extremely low mortality rates.[10] Since such insurance is expensive or even unobtainable at advanced ages, the long-term protection of his wife's financial position more properly rests on the addition of level-premium straight life insurance or even annuity and endowment policies as the breadwinner's income and financial commitments permit. The savings features of such policies, and their advantages under estate taxation, provide a degree of security that the young may simply be unable to afford but that the slightly older couple may find maximizes their attempts at rational long-term timing of the family as an economic entity.

The rate at which children are "accumulated" has continuing and not just temporary implications for the temporal ordering of family life. The parents who hope to give their children, and especially the boys, the best possible start in life may tardily realize that the short interval between children, for whatever reasons, has potentially adverse implications for the expenses of higher education some years later. This realization, in turn, may have a major effect on the form and rate of savings that the family will attempt. Similarly, the father of closely spaced daughters may find weddings at his expense in rapid succession, with considerable damage to the family's liquid resources. If the girls have also had college educations, it may take years for the family to return to some measure of financial stability.

Although youths may have to wait long for family inheritance, the expenses of a higher education borne by parents are properly viewed as a kind of "hidden capital transfer," as the educational investment is likely to have a substantial effect on young men's further earning power and probably a favorable effect on young women's chances for a husband with above-average income prospects.

The family's outlays on their children's education can thus be considered a kind of preinheritance. Among the relatively well-to-do, and perhaps with some frequency among lower economic groups also, the young married couple may also be given other financial assistance. Often this assistance will be in the form of a real or nominal loan, though with little or no interest. The loan preserves the convention of the independence of the generations and avoids at least temporarily the question of any ultimate distribution of property among heirs. The loan may also provide a kind of contractual assurance of support of the parents in old age by the "borrower" if they should unexpectedly need it. When an outright gift is made, it appears more likely to come from the husband's parents than from the wife's. In this case the concept of the "male dowry" immediately suggests itself.

The purchase of a home is perhaps the major concentrated expense of a family, since most mortgage arrangements (except for some ex-servicemen and the customers of some builders of low-cost and "mass-produced" houses) require something like 20 per cent or more of the total cost as an initial payment. It appears probable, again on the basis of scanty evidence, that part of the rapid expansion of home ownership since World War II [11] has in effect represented preinheritance or a "male dowry," even though the young couple's initial equity has come from the husband's middle-aged parents in the nominal form of a loan.

If we view the "family" only as the "family of procreation," [12] formed by the marriage of youths or young adults, then its typical stages are three: the relatively short childless stage after marriage, the major stage in terms of time (and family functions) when one or more immature children are in the home, and a shorter but possibly substantial period—the stage of the "empty nest," when the couple is once more effectively childless. The length of these stages will be affected by custom, by the biology of reproduction, and by the individual life spans. The major potential components of deliberate control of the temporal order are the age of marriage and the possibility of family planning—numbers of children and their spacing—through one form or another of birth control.

Yet despite some important normative elements in industrial

societies that make of the two-generational unit *the* family, it is evident that the family is also properly viewed as a multigenerational entity. That perspective, though not eliminating the importance of the nuclear family's cycle and its many problems of sequence and timing, adds a longer time horizon and places its temporal structure in a changing historical setting. Long lineages and an extremely long-term view of such matters as family property are understandably uncommon in the changeful social structures of industrial societies, but greater longevity has tended to retain or restore a kind of "timeless" (or at least long-time) orientation to the family as an enduring organization.

NOTES

1. See Wilbert E. Moore, "Sociological Aspects of American Socialist Theory and Practice," in Donald Drew Egbert and Stow Persons, eds., *Socialism in American Life* (Princeton: Princeton University Press, 1952), Vol. I, Chapter 11, especially "Radical Parties," pp. 549–552; also, Erving Goffman, *Asylums* (Garden City: Doubleday Anchor, 1961), especially "On the Characteristics of Total Institutions."

2. See, for example, William F. Ogburn and Meyer F. Nimkoff, *Sociology* (Boston: Houghton Mifflin, 1940), pp. 713–715; Nimkoff, *Marriage and the Family* (Boston: Houghton Mifflin, 1947), pp. 92–94; Reuben Hill, "Plans for Strengthening Family Life," in Howard Becker and Reuben Hill, eds., *Marriage and Parenthood* (Boston: Heath, 1948), p. 779.

3. Sebastian de Grazia, "The Uses of Time," in Robert Kleemeier, ed., *Aging and Leisure* (New York: Oxford University Press, 1961), Chapter 5, statistics from pp. 123–125. See also his *Of Time, Work and Leisure* (New York: Twentieth Century Fund, 1962), especially Appendix tables, pp. 441–475.

4. *Ibid.*

5. Paul Fraisse, "Of Time and the Worker," *Harvard Business Rev.*, 37: 121–125, May/June 1959.

6. Paul C. Glick, *American Families* (New York: Wiley, 1957), p. 195.

7. Gary S. Becker, "An Economic Analysis of Fertility," in National Bureau of Economic Research, *Demographic and Economic Change in Developed Countries* (Princeton: Princeton University Press, 1960).

8. Charles F. Westoff and others, *Family Growth in Metropolitan America* (Princeton: Princeton University Press, 1961), p. 127. For data on the timing of births see Chapter VI, "Birth Intervals," and Chapter VII, "Preferred Birth Intervals."

9. See Paul C. Glick, *op. cit.*, pp. 54–55.

10. See, for example, Judson T. Landis and Mary G. Landis, *Building a Successful Marriage*, 3rd ed. (New York: Prentice Hall, 1958), Chapter 21; also, Norman E. Himes, *Your Marriage* (New York: Rinehart, 1940), Chapters 17 and 18.

11. The proportion of owner occupancy of all occupied dwelling units has changed as follows:

1890	47.8 per cent
1940	43.6 per cent
1950	55.0 per cent
1960	61.9 per cent

See U. S. Department of Commerce, Bureau of the Census, *U. S. Census of Housing, 1950*, Vol. I, p. xxx; and *U. S. Census of Housing, 1960*, Advance Reports, Series HC(A1)-52, p. 2.

12. For the development of the distinction between "family of orientation" and "family of procreation," see W. Lloyd Warner, "A Methodology for the Study of the Development of Family Attitudes," *Soc. Sci. Res. Council Bull.*, No. 18, 28–34, June 1933.

Five

Administrative Organization

In contrast to the family, with its residual claims on the time of many of its members, the work organization is a primary and even peremptory claimant. The civilian governmental agency, the private business corporation, the administrative staff of the school or hospital, even the national headquarters of labor unions share a common form of organization. Except for its custodial features, with the attendant "total" claim on and responsibility for members' time, the military organization is a highly developed model of the type. In sociological shorthand the organizational type is known as "bureaucracy," [1] without the negative connotation commonly associated with the term (or the improper limitation of negative features to public agencies). In slightly more cumbersome but less ambiguous language the category may be identified as the administrative organization.

The essential features of administrative organization of present relevance may be briefly enumerated: (1) limited and ordered objectives, to be achieved by (2) rational procedures and (3) rational selection and allocation of personnel for whom (4) membership is a livelihood. A number of other organizational characteristics follow from these specifications. Precise policies and objectives are formulated, procedures (and their associated rules of conduct) are established, and participants are recruited on the basis of a hierarchy of authority. That authority is also responsible for maintaining discipline and for the maintenance of stable or adaptive relations with the organization's significant environment. Complex specialization and precise specifications of duties and their boundaries require coordination, which in turn involves both *synchronization* and *sequence* of actions and an elaborate communicative network that supplies information for action and decision, differentiated by source, route, and destination.

The administrative organization is perhaps man's most impressive social invention, and it has become also the major instrumentality for the control and use of man's nonhuman environment. Although the "purity" of the structural type is highly correlated with organizational size, substantial elements of the complex model may be found in administrative units that afford only two echelons of authority—the "boss," two or more supervisors, and a number of workers of one sort or another. Significant traces of the "pure" type are to be found wherever a worker or salaried employee "reports" to a superior, for the discipline of employment includes a discipline of time. By that extended sense of administrative organizations they comprise the locus of livelihood, the organization of production of goods and services, for a great majority of the breadwinners in industrial societies; well over four fifths of the workers in the United States and all workers in Soviet-type economies are at least nominally "bureaucratized." Certainly considerably more than half of all those gainfully occupied in industrial societies work in organizations large enough to present all the essential features of the structural type.

The temporal features of administrative organizations, as in other social systems, include time as a finite supply or boundary condition and the various aspects of synchronization, sequence, and rate of activities. It is the complexity of administrative systems that gives these dimensions of time special significance.

The Temporal Assets of Administrative Organizations

Administrative organizations provide an excellent example of the utility, for social analysis, of dealing with idealized models and then permitting various realistic imperfections to enter the picture. The importance of the ideal model derives from two sources, which from time to time are interrelated. One source is the development and perfection by sociological theorists of the specifications of the organizational type and the analysis of the interrelation of structural features in a complex system of action. For the theorists and the systematic observer the model provides both a checklist of actions to be noted and a pattern for tracing through the implications of observed "imperfections," of departures of one sort or another in operating organizations. The model, however, is not simply academic and therefore alien to organizers and practitioners; it also constitutes a standard or approximation and a set of criteria for judging performance.

Employers' Inventories of Time

The temporal assets of ideal administrative organizations are highly precise both in their totals and their distributions. The mission or objectives of the organization, including the magnitude of the operation, constitute the initial determinant of the structure necessary for success—the end indeed "justifies" the means, at least in any system that presupposes rational procedures for achieving goals. Alternative procedures may still be available, but if certain variables are taken as given—for example, the physical technology of industrial production, the sizes of classes in a school system, the optimal number of direct subordinates (span of control) for any coordinating supervisor, the number of hours of the standard workday or workweek—the "manning tables" may be thought of as determined, a derivative of a dependent variable in an arithmetic problem with a relatively simple and finite solution. For a freshly constructed organization the computation of manpower needs will yield a shopping list of varieties and quantities of workers to be sought on the labor market (or requisitioned from some reserve inventory of workers, as in military organizations and totalitarian economies).

The assumptions made to arrive at so simple a solution are clearly unrealistic in a number of significant ways. The variables assumed as "given" may in fact be subject to discretionary change. If the persons with appropriate skills and in the "necessary" numbers are simply not available, or not available at the market price or within the financial or political resources of the prospective employer, some alternative solution will be required, including possibly even the redefinition of the mission and its magnitude. Machines may be substituted for men, the size of classes enlarged or substandard teachers hired, or managers "stretched" by widening their spheres of responsibility.

The assumption of rationality itself cannot be accepted as unproblematical. Myth, tradition, or sentiment may intrude in the calculus of decision—the determination of what should be done and who should do it. Rational conduct also presupposes relevant knowledge, a reasonable certainty in the relation between action and objectively verifiable results. In a great many situations this knowledge is not available to those making organizational decisions, or it is not available anywhere. The achievement of certain objectives may be extremely difficult to verify—for example, a favorable "public image" for a business corporation or the lasting effect of education—and even if verifiable the procedures leading to them may have been based on trial, error, and perhaps "accidental" (perhaps even nonrepeatable) success.

The purport of these realistic imperfections in administrative organizations is that the time inventories are by no means so determinate as the ideal model would indicate. The actual temporal assets always reflect in part the fallible judgment of administrative authorities and not just the necessary, almost mechanical solution to a set of mechanical problems. The fact of employment of certain numbers of people for a nominally definite number of hours gives an empirical solution to the question of temporal assets, but that solution will differ in unknown amounts from the unattainable "ideal." The organization, in other words, may be overstaffed or understaffed without its being evident except at the extremes at which adverse affects on costs and objectives become recognizable. Even the pragmatic solution is subject to uncertainty and error—for example, variations in employment levels over periods of time or fluctuations in the number of absentees who are not immediately replaced by substitutes.

Units of Organizational Time

The "standard" workday and workweek may contain fictional elements, which are somewhat more challenging than the not very meaningful aggregate of organizational time. Though time is a continuous variable, it is commonly divided into conventional standardized units. Some activities at work may be measured in minutes or even microseconds, but for various administrative purposes, including the notable one of compensation, units ranging from the hour to the year are used, and the workday affects virtually every employee regardless of method of compensation. Yet a unit of that length sharply reduces flexibility of calculating necessary temporal assets. It would indeed be remarkable if the scale of operations and the organization of tasks could be translated into a number of man-hours (or minutes or seconds) so precise that they totaled to an even number of man-days, to say nothing of having an even total for each distinct job or set of role specifications assignable to a single individual. Part-time workers may or may not be available "in the market," and in any event their employment runs up overhead costs per man-hour. Compensated overtime work may also add a measure of flexibility. It is inevitable, however, that some assignments will end up being "easy" in terms of the activities required per unit of time and others will require either greater speed or longer work or both.

Limits on Temporal Flexibility

Were man-hours truly additive, a simple question of manning jobs with completely interchangeable performers, the temporal needs of organizations would be far easier to determine and the flexibility of implementation at the maximum. Aside from temporal flexibilities as such—adding or subtracting time or changing activity rates—administrative organizations do afford several common types of latitude in assignment. Such latitude is usually, but not always, an organizational device for handling emergencies rather than "normal operations."

Because of training time, occupational transferability has a generally negative correlation with level of skills. The unskilled worker has, almost by definition, an extremely wide range of specific occupations as long as the job requirements entail only simple directions or a quick demonstration. The aggregate demand for unskilled workers has steadily decreased as machines have replaced muscles, but virtually all administrative organizations offer employment to one or more "handymen" who are assigned a wide variety of tasks during the day or week. Since none of the tasks constitutes a "full-time" job, the worker's transferability avoids a whole succession of part-time workers or "contracting out" to some kind of independent "service organization."

Some "emergency" flexibility is also provided by the possibility of some movement "up" or "down" in the same line of skills and experience. Thus the foreman promoted from the ranks may be able to take over the job of an absent subordinate and an assistant manager may be made "acting" chief of a bureau. To the degree that all tasks are increasingly specialized and not simply "divided" or "duplicated," subordinates in an administrative sense may be "superior" in technical performance and at the same time gain no experience in coordination, with the result that "vertical" interchange becomes almost impossible.

The administrative organization therefore commands temporal assets that are somewhat less finite and determinate than would be true of the ideal model. Yet by comparison with most other organizations, the time inventory is remarkably exact. Paradoxically, the closer the concrete organization approaches the ideal in one respect—a degree of specialization of positions *and of the qualities of their incumbents* that yields no duplication or close affinity —the more exact will be the temporal inventory and the less sensible will be any attempt to make the units additive. It is the closeness with which concrete organizations approach that state of affairs that makes the problem of temporal coordination acute.

The fixing of an administrative organization's long-term temporal assets is complicated by organizational immortality. Of course, not all organizations actually endure for long periods. Business corporations may fail and governmental agencies may be abolished. Intentional temporal limits are, however, rather rare. Cases may occur in which an organization is assembled for a finite rather than a continuous task—such as an army fighting a war but disbanded with the cessation of hostilities—or established for a limited calendar period—for example, a singular five-year construction program. But for the enduring and nominally eternal structure the ideal model provides no answer at all to the question of long-term restraints, for in that model the organization precedes all contemporary participants (at least as a planned structure) and is normally designed to endure beyond their tenancy. The organization is thus somewhat analogous to an entire society: hiring is equivalent to childbirth and retirement, to death, and with any close approximation to the age distribution of the labor force as a whole both events should be frequent or "constant" processes.

The nature of long-term restraints is in effect determined by the organization's future planning horizon (which, however, may be different for various activities). Within these somewhat arbitrary limits, temporal allocation once more involves the utilization of man-hours from current assets or changing their number and distribution according to plan, but this process is almost impossible to distinguish from sequential order and timing. For the "immortal" organization time loses its static, boundary-setting qualities over the long term, *although those qualities remain at any particular time,* in the present or the sensibly foreseeable future.

Time and Administrative Coordination

Syncronization and sequence of actions are intrinsic and prominent elements in any system of coordinated specialization. The extreme case of fine timing, or at least the extreme case that affects large numbers of workers, involves the intermeshing of human and mechanical processes. Since, in the ideal model of organization, each action is indispensable and must be performed at the right time, sequence, and rate, failure on any score is disruptive of the entire process. Hence close discipline is implied, but, realistically, some actual flexibility is also implied to prevent the entire coordinated system from being at the mercy of every participant.

The need for temporal coordination, like the specificity of man-hour requirements, tends to decrease with structural distance from machine processes, although perhaps not so sharply, since temporal interdependence is not purely determined mechanically. In some cases the machine speed is less demanding or inhibiting than the proficiency of the operator—for example, the typist or printing compositor or the operator of a factory fork-lift truck for handling materials. Yet other activities await the timely completion of tasks. The duties of other jobs may not involve machines at all—for example, issuing prompt oral instructions for a minor change in operating procedures. In other cases, and this is notably the situation of advisers and decision makers, presence and availability may be the primary criteria for temporal ordering rather than a predetermined and repetitive schedule of actions.

Sequential Ordering of Administrative Acts

The complex and indirect communicative networks of administrative organizations are especially dependent on fulfilling "expectations" with regard to both sequence and speed.[2] The information or instruction that bypasses channels violates expectations of constituted intermediaries and may be viewed by the recipients as lacking authenticity. The message that arrives "too soon," or more probably "too late," may be worse than simply disorderly; it can be disastrous. In a relatively stable situation information on "current state" may be both routine and slow. For a military battle or a highly competitive business market the updating of information may be frequent or nearly continuous. Even so, necessary time delays in altering policies and procedures, the redistribution of resources, may mean that current action is predicated on clearly superseded information. Here, in fact, we encounter a negative "bureaucratic" feature of administrative organizations, for their massive and complex interdependence makes them ill-suited to rapid alterations of course and procedures.

The Timing of Action

Administrative decentralization, which shortens the lines of communication by permitting problem solving near the organization points at which the problems occur, also reduces the time lag in reaction. If, however, decisions are carefully retained at executive level, the only way to maintain any short-term flexibility is somehow to speed the flow of essential "current state" information from the organizational unit responsible for its collection and preliminary evaluation. Thus in mid-1962 President Kennedy was reported by the press to be unhappy at the pace of information-supply by the Department of State and to be demanding some reorganization adequate to reflect the urgency the President attached to the task.[3] Even so, the finite limits on any executive's time requires substantial decentralization. Moreover, true synchronization of the flow of messages to a single recipient ceases to be communicative: it is noise. And since understanding and drawing implications for action require that the information be placed "in context," a disordered sequence of messages can lead to radically erroneous judgments.

The massive, seemingly incessant flow of communications in administrative organizations may so completely absorb an officeholder's time and attention that he will lose virtually all initiative and even find keeping up with other elements of "routine" administration impossible. Indeed, one effective way of subverting an administrator's capacity to act is to saturate his inbound communications, to "give him more information than he ever needed to know."

Administrative coordination is also challenged if it is discontinuous while parts of the organization are in continuous operation. Thus industrial plants that operate "around the clock" present the problem of providing emergency or even normal supervisory, technical, and managerial man-hours for the extra shifts. It may be whimsical to speculate about the president's office having three different occupants in twenty-four hours, but strains are likely to appear at some managerial level wherever continuous production is not continuously "managed."

A somewhat analogous problem is that of temporal coordination across substantial geographical distances. Instantaneous communication provides no answer to the circumstance that clocks are set to different "standard" times. It will be late morning or noon before a New York executive can expect to reach a plant manager at his office on the Pacific Coast, and the latter can only hope that he will have no need to seek immediate executive decision from New York headquarters after 2 P.M. For transatlantic transactions time differences may allow only a two-hour period during the normal working day in which telephone communication is possible.

"Instantaneous" communication across space is, of course, not matched by transport of persons and goods. Although air passenger and freight service may speed a missing part for repair of a machine or a repairman and materials needed for on-schedule completion of a production assignment, emergencies have a way of being unforeseen and unscheduled, so that delays may be minimized but not eliminated.

The geographical limits on temporal coordination can also be seen in other contexts. Developments in Moscow are likely to occur in the middle of the Washington night, and even those in West European capitals may find American officials at cocktails, dinner, or out for the evening. (The lack of synchronization is further accentuated by the tendency in West European capitals to start operations later, by clock time, but also to work well into the early evening.) The important point in the present context is once more that information possibly requiring administrative decision may not reach the administrator during his normal decision-making time. The result is a kind of clock-dictated decentralization. One consequence of this is likely to be an upgrading of the discretionary authority of the lesser administrator during "off hours," compared with his nominal counterpart during the standard office day. The superintendent in charge of the "graveyard shift" (early morning hours) has a rather responsible position, as have the custodians of various "night desks" in the Departments of State and Defense and the "officers of the day" in military organizations.

Temporal Strategies of Administration

National governments and business corporations share, in addition to marked similarities in administrative structures, a major concern for predicting and controlling the future. Since both types of administrative organization expect to endure "forever," the actual length of the effective future horizon itself becomes a matter of decision and uncertainty. Governmental agencies are supposed to protect and enhance the national heritage for generations still unborn (who have no votes), and corporate executives are supposed to act as temporary "trustees" for an indefinite future, in the interests of those who may own no stock at present or for customers not yet in evidence. Distant planning horizons are thus understandably rare, and the choice of those nearer itself represents an element of strategy.

The Strategy of Planning

Planning for the future represents two distinct elements, which may be identified as *teleology* and *teleonomy*. Teleology is the choice of a goal, a changed state of affairs, and the marshaling of resources and activities as the means of its achievement. Teleonomy represents the attempt to predict the uncontrolled trends of the future and to make appropriate and timely adaptations to the "inevitable." [4] The two types of future orientation may become intermixed: (*a*) when a simple forecast becomes the basis of teleological action—for example, an age-specific population projection may indicate the probability of rapid increase in the number of youths reaching normal age of marriage and investments are made in the production of construction materials; (*b*) when the secondary and tertiary consequences of planned action are predicted but not directly controlled and the course of action is modified to take advantage of positive consequences and minimize the effects of negative ones; and (*c*) when efforts are continuously bent not only to improve the predictive basis of teleonomic action but also to bring some additional elements under teleological control.

Wherever there is some basis for accumulated experience in the *probability* or *risk* of error or failure, it may be possible to engage in various "averaging" techniques to spread the costs of failure through time or among a number of different organizations with comparable risks. Many kinds of insurance—for example, fire and other property loss or damage suits for civil liabilities—combine the spread of risks through time and among different participants who share common hazards.

Temporal strategies, of varying duration, are a major component of planning. Five-year plans in controlled economies do not exactly answer the problem but do reduce the strain on the industrial executive involved in the choice of interval. In competitive economic systems temporal strategies require decisions on resources (money and time) to be devoted to research, product development, market expansion, and, indeed, a host of other managerial concerns. And, since trends external to the organization are matters for prediction, with possibilities of error rather than control, the consequences of decisions may be on-phase or badly timed. It is a commonplace that effective short-run actions may have adverse long-run consequences and vice versa.

The choice of planning horizons may not be entirely arbitrary. Some relatively short-term goals may be such that there is no possible or financially feasible means of achieving them on schedule because of the relatively inelastic sequence of temporal phases necessary to reach them. If a goal is, in fact, urgent, then its time of achievement can be set only by the minimum time required to take the necessary intermediate steps.

The construction of any transportation timetable is instructive in this connection. A timetable requires prediction and control of the running time of vehicles. During the Eighteenth Century stagecoaches came into fairly general use in England and Western Europe and in the American colonies where roads permitted. The schedules, however, were highly approximate. Coaches were advertised to start, "God willing," at *about* such and such a time, "as shall seem good to a majority of the passengers," and overnight stops were also decided by vote.[5] Yet, before the railroad age, the "wonder stage," established in 1825 for the run from Shrewsbury to London, was so punctual that residents on the route regulated their watches by its arrival in town.[6]

A schedule may be constructed "backward," leading to the designation of a necessary starting time for the first of a sequence of actions in order to arrive at the destination promptly; or it may be constructed "forward," with an "estimated time of arrival" after a stipulated start. Although planning "backward" from a dated goal is extremely popular in such strategic problems as national "development planning," it has clear and severe limits. Reaching the destination on time may require more time than remains, and no amount of quickened pace can compensate for the fact that the past is history and not recoverable. The situation may well become one for which the punch line of an ancient joke is apt: "you can't get there from here."

For administrative planning in the economically underdeveloped areas of the world it is clearly not necessary to recapitulate either the sequence or rate of historical development in the advanced countries. Yet certain fairly intrinsic time lags cannot be avoided. If the national aims include universal public education, the first strategic priority in personnel is likely to be the training of teachers of teachers, so that eventually teachers can be trained to educate the children. The "built-in lag" in expanding educational facilities may thus be a decade or two.

Over a shorter but still significant time period a new product will first require the design and construction of new machines for its manufacture; a new policy of language training or diplomatic representatives will require the time necessary to acquire the language in question, if indeed the necessary teachers are available.

The strategy of planning thus involves the crucial element of *lead time*, and that time may in fact be almost impossible to predict precisely, either because the novelty of the undertaking means that parts of the sequential process are without applicable precedent or because the effect of uncontrolled events cannot be adequately predicted. For many economic or political strategies it is both important and impossible to know the future timetable —the various "running times" necessary to reach an orderly succession of destinations.

The plumbing contractor bidding on a construction job has as much need to forecast the labor time necessary to complete the job, on schedule and solvently, as the designers of spacecraft need to know the temporal "expectations" for technical innovations. The plumber's problem may be easier and less consequential for science and politics, but it is of the same general variety as that of the chief of the "space agency" or the corporate contractor.

The longer the time period to be planned, and thus the more complex the sequential series of implementing activities, the greater the possibilities of error in both teleology and teleonomy. Yet the advantage of the short term is not entirely one-sided, for there is some chance that over the long term errors may be partly balanced, an underestimate of time for one phase being offset by an unduly pessimistic allowance for another. Yet errors may also be cumulative; for example, when a small delay in early stages loses a place on subsequent production schedules, to be regained only after other priorities have been fulfilled. Tardiness by a day or two in the scheduled delivery of a manuscript to the printer may result in a delay of months in publication. A manufacturer who is a "late entrant" into a product market may find all normal distribution channels already saturated, and additional time and expense will be required if he is to develop new ones.

The Urgency of Action

One outstanding implication of the problems of forecasting and planning is that ignorance, and the time needed to remove it by analysis and experience, is a major restraint on "perfect" control. Eels and Walton write, somewhat optimistically: "the effort to anticipate time, to lead it rather than be dragged along by it, may be perfected by a society dedicated to progress and so completely in control of change that time will have small significance." [7] Yet these authors also concede that time is a delaying element in the perfection of technology.[8] Indeed, the failure to be fully prepared, for whatever reasons, often leads to decisional urgency that cannot await development of "proper" information. This is one of the many identifiable sources of strain between the "intellectual" (the scientist or other professional) and the manager in administrative organizations.[9] The expert is not accustomed to the "terrible immediacy" of administrative decision and when asked for advice based on reliable knowledge does not welcome the additional note, "We needed it yesterday."

The story is told of the member of some national parliament who, in preparation for a major address to the assembly, sought information from a seemingly appropriate governmental agency. The bureaucrat informed the legislator that if the parliament had approved the last requested budget the agency might have had the information available. Under the circumstances it would take six months and money and personnel not available to do the necessary research. The representative went off disgruntled, and the bureaucrat attended the following day's session to see how his disappointed client would handle the situation. To the civil servant's dismay, the speaker's presentation was heavily buttressed with appropriate descriptive data and statistics. At the end of the speech he caught the politician and asked how he got his information. "Didn't you say it would take six months to get the facts?" "Yes, at least." "Well, I estimate it would take that long for anyone to prove me wrong."

Wherever the demand for information exceeds the timely supply, as it does in many decisional contexts, administrative and otherwise, spurious "information" and ignorant action are likely to follow.[10] If the outcome of action is sufficiently far ahead in time and the action situation sufficiently complex, it may not even be possible to identify the ignorance and error. Uncertainties and errors give rise to new attempts to increase the certainty of an uncertain world. And if the inconsistency between effective control and the felt need for it produces magical solutions, as such situations do universally,[11] it also produces constant attempts to reduce the area of uncertainty.

Rivals and competitors may be among the uncontrolled elements in an administrative organization's significant environment. (This may be true even of nominally coordinated structures, such as governmental agencies or divisions of corporation.) The most obvious strategic use of time in such situations is speed. To be first in the market with a product, the first jurisdictional claimant for a new function, or ahead in the "weapons race" constitutes a strategic advantage. About the only advantages of delay (and these may at times be rationalizations for conspicuous tardiness) are that the planning has been sounder and thus more effective or more durable, that one may profit from his opponent's mistakes, or even profit from his successes if they can be readily copied and then more quickly improved than he is likely to do in view of inflexibilities in his equipment and other investments.

Occasionally advantage may be taken of a rival's known periodic schedule. Thus it has been claimed that Hitler, before World War II, made his major moves in violation of treaties and territories on week ends, mainly because of his knowledge of the "long weekend" practiced by British cabinet ministers and their consequent incompetence to take any prompt diplomatic countermeasures.[12] Even flexible opportunism may be practiced. The ideological sympathy of an American corporation's managers for their competitor whose workers are on strike may not deter him from attempting to capture and hold a larger share of their market. University graduate schools in their competition for the most highly qualified students may surreptitiously violate the agreed-on "release date" of invitations and financial offers, just as the preradio newspaper reporter attempted to score a "scoop."

It seems obvious that a highly centralized and indeed autocratic organization can take quick and massive action impossible for one that is decentralized or encumbered with democratic accountabilities. The flexibility is only partial, however. It is especially weak in securing timely action on relatively small operating problems, and failures may be cumulative. Hitler could order the invasion of the Soviet Union without elaborate prior discussion, but he could not be reached to authorize timely reinforcements against the Allied invasion of Normandy.

Size too has its penalties along with its powers. A small manufacturer may be able to change his price list almost daily in a competitive market, whereas the large corporation may require months of lead time just to prepare the necessary forms for the printer.

The future, though partially predictable and even somewhat subject to deliberate control, still offers significant surprises. Thus, inevitably, some temporal strategies will be effective because of proper foresight and efficient implementation, and some will simply be lucky. Just as critics tend to blame administrators for errors beyond their control, so administrators tend to take undue credit for good guesses. Perhaps in some grand scheme of things a crude approximation to a just balance will result.

NOTES

1. The classic formulation of the characteristics of bureaucracy was that of Max Weber. See his *Theory of Social and Economic Organization*, translated by A. M. Henderson and Talcott Parsons (New York: Oxford University Press, 1947), pp. 329–341. For a more contemporary treatment, representing considerable modifications of Weber's model and applied primarily to the industrial corporation, see Wilbert E. Moore,

The Conduct of the Corporation (New York: Random House, 1962), especially Chapters 2–6.

2. See Moore, *op. cit.*, Chapter 5, "Now Hear This."
3. *The New York Times*, July 3, 1962, p. 1.
4. See Arnold S. Feldman and Wilbert E. Moore, "Industrialization and Industrialism: Convergence and Differentiation," in *Trans. Fifth World Cong. Sociology*, Washington, 1962, Vol. II, pp. 151–169, especially pp. 168–169.

Stanley Stark distinguishes between rational problem solving in a closed system, which he characterizes as requiring "atemporal" foresight, and rational action in a situation of change and uncertainty, requiring "temporal" foresight. See Stanley Stark, "Temporal and Atemporal Foresight," University of Illinois, Institute of Labor and Industrial Relations, Reprint Series 117 (1962).

5. H. O. Duncan, *The World on Wheels* (Paris: author, no date), pp. 23–24.
6. See Stanley Harris, *The Old Coaching Age* (London: Richard Bentley & Son, 1885), pp. 3–4.
7. Richard Eels and Clarence Walton, *Conceptual Foundations of Business* (Homewood, Ill.: Richard D. Irwin, 1961), p. 419.
8. *Ibid.*, pp. 412–413.
9. See Robert K. Merton, *Social Theory and Social Structure*, rev. ed. (Glencoe, Ill.: Free Press, 1957), Chapter VIII, "The Role of the Intellectual in Public Bureaucracy."
10. See Moore, *op. cit.*, especially pp. 69–74.
11. See Bronislaw Malinowski, *Magic, Science and Religion* (Glencoe, Ill.: Free Press, 1948), pp. 11–16; also, Malinowski, "Culture," in *Encyclopedia of the Social Sciences* (New York: Macmillan, 1931), Vol. IV, pp. 634–640.
12. See William L. Shirer, *The Rise and Fall of the Third Reich* (Greenwich: Fawcett Publications, 1962), pp. 391, 413.

Six

Voluntary Associations

To the extent that various organizations established to promote one interest or another are voluntary in membership, the most immediate and obvious temporal dimension in their conduct is that of time scarcity deriving from competition for the limited supplies available. Synchronization of activities and their sequence and rate also present problems somewhat peculiar to this type of organization, but these problems seem secondary compared with the fundamental difficulty of securing an inventory of disposable time.

Though by no means unknown in primitive and agrarian societies, the association appears to be functionally related to organizational specialization of such major social activities as production and government and the multiplication of intersecting interests. Not least among the factors conducive to associational activity is the demarcation between mandatory and residual or discretionary time that organizational specialization, built around crucial social functions, brings in its train.

The United States is sometimes said to be a nation of joiners. The characterization has some approximation to fact, but it is not very distinguishing. There is nothing peculiar about American "national character" that leads to a proliferation of special-interest associations. Such associations are typical of at least the urban sectors of all industrial societies, and with the progress of industrialization rural-urban differences tend to diminish.

The number of associations and the extent of participation in them are variable from one country to another, it is true, according to national legal and political structure. "Freedom of association" is essentially a common-law conception of liberty; the more "codified" regulatory system of Roman law tends to a greater extension of political supervision over associations even in nominally pluralistic and democratic societies such as those of Western Europe.[1] In totalitarian regimes there is no dearth of associations; on the contrary. What is basically questionable in those political systems is the qualifier "voluntary." The associations that are permitted to exist openly and officially must have aims consistent with the established political and social doctrine. Given these qualifications, associations are not simply permitted: they are encouraged and, in a sense, "established." Then by manipulation of "peer-group pressure," coupled if necessary with strong elements of overt coercion by party or other officials, the individual is "encouraged" to volunteer for participation. The degree of official exhortation to the citizen to use his time constructively, to improve his mind and body, and to join in civic construction [2] strongly suggests that the administrative costs of persuasion are less than the costs of terror and that neither has succeeded in removing at least the residual liberty of nonparticipation, the "right to be apathetic."

When participation in associations is truly optional, these organizations occupy a "residual" position in individual life organization different in a sense from that of the family's temporal claims. Clearly the association occupies a much lower rank than the family in social valuation, and this rankorder is almost certain to be represented in actual time allotments. The family, however, is residual in another and less derogatory sense: it claims all time (and energy, affection, or other scarce resources) not specifically and honorably allocated elsewhere. Except for the demands of work and school, the family member who is "completely wrapped up" in family affairs may be regarded as unwise but not immoral. The person who becomes "married" to an association may be regarded as neglectful of duties with a higher priority, though the condemnation may be softened or removed if the activity is religious or otherwise uplifting.

Uneven Temporal Resources of Associations

The association, though "residual" in its low-priority claim on time, may also be said to be "intermediate" between the fairly firm schedule of the work organization or school and the rather open-ended claims of the family. But the "association" rarely presents itself to the individual in the singular. The number of associations available and the degree of their specialization is naturally correlated with the size of the community. However, even if most social life revolves around the church or the school for the rural or small-town family, these organizations will turn out to be multifunctional and internally specialized, the formal organization serving in part as a kind of holding company or perhaps only as the spatial location for activities having little to do with religion or education.

The Competition for Time

If we argue from the "pure" case (which may be widely approximated only in countries sharing the Anglo-American legal system), associations are voluntary in the dual sense that any membership at all is optional and that a choice is available among associations. Like leisure in general—and it is from leisure time that associational time is drawn—participation is *discretionary*.

The limited-interest quality of associations is another way of saying that they are functionally specialized. A distinction has been drawn between groups with preclusive memberships and those that may compete for the temporal resources of common members. This distinction has a high though not perfect coincidence with a fundamental duality in the nature of associations. Some are organized to promote the common aspirations of members for protected or increased income and power; these are "interest groups" in the proper and restricted sense of the term. The second type of association may be designated as "expressive," though the purposes of group action may range from the grandly philanthropic to the trivially playful, from the austerely religious to the raucously convivial.[3]

An interest group tends to be preclusive in its membership with regard to the issue or range of issues that its charter proclaims, though overlapping interests occur. Since the organizations are essentially competitive or conflicting in orientation, only a spy or a pretty silly joiner would become identified with two or more contestants. For expressive associations, on the other hand, an individual's potential memberships need to be limited only by the range of his enthusiasms and his scarce resources, notably including time.

The division, of course, is by no means tidy. Because both types of association draw from the same pool of discretionary time, interest groups are competitive with expressive ones with regard to time, though not with one another within the narrow range of their special missions. And the narrower the definition of the collective interest, the more such groups an individual may "reasonably" join. Interest groups (and, indeed, others) have a way of extending their scope, or generalizing and elaborating their "package" of values to be pursued. It is accordingly a fairly old bit of sociological wisdom to note that many individuals tend to belong to groups that profess inconsistent values. It would be improperly cynical to assert that such value inconsistency is consequential only if it results in role conflict—inconsistent behavorial expectations in a particular context of action at a particular time. Individuals, after all, may reflect on their values and seek something like an orderly "value set" as well as a feasible "role set." An individual may, in fact, come to recognize a value inconsistency among his group affiliations by hypothetical role playing—the "mental experiment" in a potential *contretemps*.

Yet, given the scarcity of time and energy, the probability of role conflict for the multiple joiner is somewhat more than abstract and hypothetical.

The competitive claims of associations are further complicated by the interplay between organizational objectives and the individual's motives for joining and participating. The individual may join a genuine interest group defensively, that is, to protect interests potentially threatened by the activities of other diverse interests. If organized activity becomes the norm for the competitive pursuit of particular political or economic interests, the one liberty the sensible individual may lose irretrievably is the option of remaining "unorganized." [4] MacIver and Page note that many associations are not based on common interests—". . . when two or more persons seek a goal or objective which is one and indivisible for them all . . ."—but on like interests—". . . when two or more persons severally or distributively pursue a like object or value, each for himself. . . ." [5] In both cases, but particularly in the second, collective action is merely instrumental. Instrumental orientations, however, may be more far-reaching: the association may be useful to the individual for his aspirations to elective political office, for the professional "contacts" (and thus potential clients) that it affords, or as a kind of expected and prestige service to be performed by a business leader or by the "society" debutante who may have to pretend to be charitably disposed and socially useful.

To the degree that associational membership is a fairly mandatory component of social position, the notion of voluntary participation is more than faintly impaired, and we are right back where we were in Chapter 2 with respect to leisure as "discretionary" time. Once more, however, if any associational membership is somewhat optional, and there are genuine alternatives in the choice of particular groups with which the individual may become identified, we are, in fact, dealing with a "probabilistic" and not an absolutely "deterministic" system. From the point of view of associations, time inventories then become problematic and possibly variable rather than a simple result of a "captive clientele" of a certain size. Even if some memberships are fairly reliable and derivative, they may be nominal and *pro forma* and thus add more to membership rolls than to the actual assets of usable time.

The competition among associations for memberships and time is accentuated rather than relieved by the social selection of "high participators." As also noted in Chapter 2, it is precisely those who are not "alienated" from work (or, presumably, from the family) who comprise the active joiners. Unless we make the cynical assumption that all this activity is simply in furtherance of career goals, it would appear that the joiners have a wider range of interests than others. Although direct evidence is not available, it might be expected that a disproportionate number of those with multiple memberships, the busy individuals who are "good organization people," would become identified with "common" and not just "like" interests. The goals (or other rewards) offered by the association must provide *salience* (relevance and value [6]) to the prospect for him to join at all and for him to continue to invest any substantial amount of time in its activities.

The Rise and Fall of Activities

The most probable historic course of the person-time assets of associations would be represented by a relatively short but steep initial rise in the "time-inventory curve," reflecting a combination of growing membership and initial high participation on the part of each, followed by a gradual decrease as member-hours if not actual members are reduced. A new function, a new "service" to members, or even a new urgency in the goal of a proper "interest group" may temporarily reverse the trend to be followed inevitably by a new decline. In some cases, such as the political party or club, recurrent elections may provide the environmental occasion for periodic revivals. A sustained high pitch of participation is quite unlikely, however, and any attempt to achieve it is likely to require exceptional inputs of time by some in order to provide a "never ending" supply of novel appeals.

Time, Loyalty, and Power

Once an organization is established, its continuation is likely to become an end in itself, a "common" value, for some members, even if its charter and original basis of appeal have been clearly instrumental.[6] Though strong enthusiasm for the organization may have been based originally on a judgment of high but instrumental salience on the part of some members, concern for its welfare is likely to "trap" the most active participants into identification with it as an entity.

For persons identified with the organization, the "good organizational people," participation time will be taken as an indicator and symbol of loyalty. Yet the dual and intersecting circumstances that the value attached to the organization or its goals will be unequal among members and that members have other claims on their time and loyalty lead to the expectation of a markedly differential participation rate—both at any given time and through time. The simplest way to represent differential participation is the distinction between the "active center" and the "passive periphery." A somewhat more precise representation would require the construction of a "participation scale," for which time should be a reliable indicator. Such a scale would certainly reveal that only a minority of members would comply with or approximate the association's own ideal norms of duties and activity rates.

Participation time, although indicative of loyalty, is instrumental for power. The active participant need not seek power. It will be thrust on him in the guise of "responsibility." Time may be money in the economic market place, but in the voluntary association *time is power*.

This generalization can be formalized: any limited-interest association will be under the effective control of a minority of members for whom the association has high salience. This is an extension of Michels' "iron law of oligarchy," [7] which he applied to political parties. Note that most associations in modern democratic countries are organized on democratic principles of representative government and may have a degree of "direct democracy" in the discussion and resolution of policies and issues. The fact remains that the "passive periphery" simply abdicates its nominal power. Under these circumstances a dissident but cohesive minority—for example, representatives of a radical political group—may be able to "capture" an association and change its orientations and objectives. What is needed by the challenging group is a ready supply of disposable time at least equal to that of the constituted leaders. One temporal strategy is summarized in the dictum, "Come early and vote late." For the ordinary member associational participation may thus become defensive with regard to internal organization as well as external threat.

The stage is now set for a paradox. The leaders of the association are likely to be identified with the organization and its goals and thus seek to extend the participation of members both as an indication of group loyalty and as a basis for effectiveness in the pursuit of the interests for which the association was founded. At the same time, from the point of view of power or administration, increased participation is likely at best to delay decisional processes and at worst may threaten the whole structure of leadership.[8] Thus the leaders' attempts to conserve and expand the temporal assets of associations are tainted by ambivalence. A continuous decline may presage the group's demise, but a marked increase may presage the leaders' downfall. The steady course, if it can be maintained, may also be both the safest and the most effective.

Some Temporal Strategies

Because of the normally competitive situation of associations, both among themselves and with other time-demanding social activities, and because at least some associational activities are assembled, an organization seeking to attract and hold participating members must somehow find a common place on diverse schedules. For any new association some potential participants are almost certain to disqualify themselves on the basis of other commitments. If such temporally disqualified persons are sufficiently numerous, or particular individuals among them are thought to be crucial for the organization's success, the proposed meeting times may have to be changed to accommodate them or the project abandoned entirely. Religious groups have prior claims on certain times, supported by ancient traditions, but they may have difficulty, despite their high "value-priority," in scheduling midweek meetings. Housewives generally have more discretionary time during the day, when husbands are at work and children at school. Evenings and week ends normally comprise the "free time" of employed men, but, aside from possible church attendance, the week end is likely to be reserved for family-oriented activities. An "emergency" meeting on the week end might be attended, but not a regular one, even if the frequency is, say, monthly. For associations seeking participation of both husbands and wives, the mother of immature children must usually get a baby-sitter, and this expense means that the balance sheet of costs and benefits is altered: the salience of the association must be high to secure participation.

The hour of the day as well as the day of the week is thus a problem in strategy, which obviously differs according to the intended clientele. Various "service clubs," with membership comprised mainly of business and professional men, have midday meetings for lunch, since most members in communities of substantial size probably do not go home to lunch anyway. Women's garden and reading clubs may also lunch together for complementary reasons. "Dinner meetings" are rather rare if they do not include both husbands and wives, for the symbolism of meals as "family-oriented" remains strong, even if commonly neglected at midday and possibly even at breakfast in households in which starting schedules for the day are varied. In suburban communities with a considerable proportion of commuting males, associations that hope to secure their attendance at meetings must schedule sessions late enough to permit the commuter to have dinner at home and must adjourn early enough to permit him to get his night's sleep before an early start the next day.

The frequency of meetings is also clearly a matter for decision. To the hesitant prospect, the time cost of frequent meetings may be regarded as prohibitive, yet the promise of infrequent meetings may belie the enthusiasm or urgency of the recruiter's extolling the virtues of membership. The annual meetings of national associations may include only elected delegates (the "good organization people" again) from local units, or, if it is a full "membership" meeting, attendance must be optional (because of competing obligations) and may be small. The effective strength of such associations is likely to rest on large investments of time by the active minority, written communications (magazines and "newsletters"), and perhaps local or "chapter" meetings monthly or even more often.

Over the longer term, too, temporal strategies may be precarious. The appeal of an association to prospects and many members may well be the finite and early realizable aim of collective action.[9] Political life offers many examples of the specific and dated goal: winning a particular election, prevention of a particular proposal for a change in the zoning code, or mustering support for a new playground.

Again, however, we encounter inconsistent temporal perspectives. For the leaders, the people who become committed to the organization and identified with it, success in the organization's finite mission is disastrous. For the continuity of such organizations, nothing succeeds like failure or, perhaps, near success, a close enough approximation to victory to keep the issue or party alive and to keep a sufficient number of supporters to justify associational activity. The leaders of some "protest" organizations (such as some labor unions and "radical" political parties) may utilize the old sociological principle that an external enemy will increase the internal solidarity or cohesion of a group and "bloody the troops" by entering a contest in which the organization is foredoomed to defeat. This, however, is a risky strategy, since it will work only if the common interest or other basis of salience of group membership is sufficient to ensure that defeat will not simply mean dissolution. The strategy may not withstand an unrelieved succession of collective defeats.

Although the birth rate of associations in industrial societies is high, "natural increase" is dampened by high mortality. Some defunct associations may have had a short but successful life. Others simply failed, not only in their mission but also in holding the loyalty of their members. The hardy survivors will include many who have rather vague and elastic objectives and a capacity to invent new ones and quietly abandon the old. In a highly changeful environment the capacity for adaptation is a requisite for even a modest approximation to associational immortality.

NOTES

1. See Arnold M. Rose, *Sociology* (New York: Knopf, 1956), Chapter 10, "Voluntary Associations," particularly Part A, "Conditions for Development," pp. 305–309; also Rose, *Theory and Method in the Social Sciences* (Minneapolis: University of Minnesota Press, 1954), Chapter 4, "Voluntary Associations in France."
2. See Harold L. Wilensky, "The Uneven Distribution of Leisure: The Impact of Economic Growth on 'Free Time,'" *Social Problems*, 9, 32–56, Summer 1961, especially p. 52.
3. For a different approach to a classification of "interests" (in a broad sense) around which associations may be formed see R. M. MacIver and Charles H. Page, *Society* (New York: Rinehart, 1949), Chapter 17, "Associations and Interests," especially pp. 443–449.
4. This was pointed out by Wilbert E. Moore in an unpublished paper, "The Place of the Individual in a Highly Organized Society," presented as the presidential address at the Eastern Sociological Society in 1953.
5. MacIver and Page, *op. cit.*, p. 440.
6. *Ibid.*, pp. 440–441.
7. See Robert Michels, *Political Parties*, translated by Eden Paul and Adar Paul (Glencoe, Ill.: Free Press, 1949).
8. This has been discussed with respect to the quest for "democracy" in labor unions by Wilbert E. Moore, "Management and Union Organization: An Analytical Comparison," in Conrad M. Arensberg and others, eds., *Research in Industrial Human Relations* (New York: Harper, 1957), pp. 119–130.
9. MacIver and Page, *op. cit.*, p. 448, note several types of "self-liquidating" associations.

IV

Time in Large-Scale
Systems

Seven

The City

The tempo of urban life has over the centuries excited comment, occasionally favorable but more often adverse. The frenetic pace of urban activity may be claimed to be conducive to creativity or its destroyer, but in either case it is portrayed as standing in sharp contrast to the measured and possibly even contemplative life of the village or countryside.

As one approaches the center of a city, the increasing concentration of persons in space appears to be matched by the increasing concentration of activities in time. Pedestrians genuinely in a hurry seem to set the pace for those who will only have to wait when they reach their destinations early. The automobile driver attempts to "make the next light," and, according to an old bit of wit, the shortest measurable time is that between the change of a traffic light to green and the horn of the car behind. Small purchases are made in feverish haste, often with monosyllabic communication. The quick cup of coffee is gulped before reporting to work, and the quick greeting is exchanged with fellow workers before getting on with a job that may not be pressing. One urges the cab driver to hurry, only to find that the plane's departure is delayed. One dashes to get aboard a subway train which will be followed in two minutes by another. The lunch appointment is made for noon or a little before in order to get a place in a restaurant already crowded with even earlier arrivals. Distance is commonly expressed in temporal rather than spatial units—two minutes from Times Square, twelve minutes from the Loop, twenty minutes from L'Opéra, an hour from Picadilly.

Urban time, like urban space, seems to become scarce because so many people are occupying it simultaneously. Yet the limits and boundaries of time, the question of time inventories, are not the outstanding features of the temporal structure of cities. In an aggregative sense, and over the short term of the day or year, the city appears to have a surfeit of man-hour units. Synchronization and sequence, the timing of activities, provide the principal sources of strain, not the careful accumulation and expenditure of a scarce resource.

In what Amos Hawley[1] calls the "independent community," typical of tribal and many peasant societies, the residential aggregation is virtually self-sufficient and its organization is likely to be encompassing and rather closely integrated. The "dependent" community—the town, city, metropolitan area in contemporary advanced societies—provides the site for most regular activities, but the activities themselves may be more closely integrated with those of the same type elsewhere than they are with other activities in the community. To a marked degree, therefore, the dependent community does not control its own destiny nor the temporal commitments of its members. The governmental or other collective activity of a community may be limited in significance for most members. Spatial localization of work and residence, and to some degree of recreation and associational participation, gives an ecological structure to the community, and one essential aspect of that structure is temporal.[2] In fact, the dependent community has a far more extensive *structure*—a set of interrelated patterns of action—than its *organization*—the roles and activities specifically related to communal goals and procedures.

Concentration and Segregation of Urban Time

The rapid pace of urban activity does not consist of unrelieved speed. The tightest temporal synchronization and sequence, Hawley notes,[3] are likely to occur during the daylight hours. Much of this concentration involves the world of work or revolves around it. The flow of traffic is greatly intensified at "rush hours," namely, the time preceding the start of business in the morning and following its cessation in the late afternoon. The shopping hours for customers are the business hours for employees in retail establishments. Business telephone calls are made mainly during office hours, and messengers and delivery men add to the flow of communication and transportation.

Yet even the concentration of work is not complete. Some activities must be "off-phase" in order to assure essential sequences, with their appropriate times. In large cities wholesale food markets reach the peak of activity in the hours between 2 and 6 A.M. Truck deliveries of other materials essential to the "normal" productive day may also be made during the night. Offices are cleaned and streets are swept most readily when they are empty. And, of course, commercial entertainment—including that major "industry" the saloon—reaches its most intense period at a time complementary to the normal working hours, chiefly the hours of the evening.

The radical temporal segregation of activities, however, tends to be blurred in the largest cities, for, as Hawley writes, "Every increase in size increases the number of individuals requiring a service at any given time." [4] Thus some eating establishments, along with motion picture theaters, service stations, coin-operated laundries, and perhaps public transportation facilities, may be open continuously. Even so, the "symmetry" is by no means complete. The population of the "central business district" and even of the entire city as a political entity varies markedly between day and night.[5] By public transportation and private automobile commuters arrive and then concentrate in the offices, shops, and factories of the city during working hours. As they leave for their homes, their places are only partly filled by customers of the city's recreational facilities. After midnight the nonresidential areas are rather sparsely populated.

Urban Pace and Rhythm

In large cities "ecological segregation" extends into the central area itself. In New York the downtown financial district and the midtown concentration of corporate offices may be nearly deserted by early evening, while the several entertainment areas are reaching their maximum daily density. If the commutation area is taken as one critical criterion of the extent of the "metropolis," then the daily and weekly rhythms may be viewed as involving a large-scale specialization of activities in time and space. The characteristic daily and weekly cycles are fairly sharply differentiated from one area to another.

The daily inbound and outbound flow of persons is primarily composed of workers, secondarily of shoppers and pleasure-seekers.[6] The weekend movement is likely to include a larger proportion of pleasure-seekers, but some city residents will also leave on the same quest at out-of-town destinations.

In cities with poorly developed rapid-transit systems from the suburbs and within their own limits (Los Angeles and Washington are notable examples in the United States) the number of man-hours spent in the "journey to work" is likely to be increased, thereby affecting the ecological structures of the cities themselves. The "decay" of the central city, which is fairly general is this country and at least partly a consequence of a reaction to automobile traffic congestion, is especially marked in metropolitan areas that rely almost exclusively on the private automobile. In those cities, and to a marked degree in all American cities, retail establishments are becoming increasingly decentralized; this presumably reduces the effective shopping time for some suburban residents. There is even some tendency to shorten the journey to work by establishing suburban business and industrial locations, but the very congestion of the city is part of its functional advantage in terms of time-space contiguities of persons and services.

Cities also have a somewhat longer rhythm of activity, especially that owing to seasonal variations. The seasonal equivalent of the daytime population of the central city is the vacation population of resort communities. The "summer people" may briefly outnumber year-round residents several times over, and to those residents the whole year has a markedly uneven pace.[7] The concentration of vacations in the summer months also affects the cities that constitute the principal sources of supply of vacationers. The extreme case is supposed to be Paris in August, which is said to be inhabited only by tourists. This is obviously an exaggeration in some unknown degree, but many cities attract nonresidents just as they temporarily repel their own, seeking a change of scene.

Temporal Complementarity

The very continuity of urban life, the demand for services around the clock and around the calendar, implies that some people must be off schedule with regard to the dominant temporal patterns. The need for protective and emergency services is neverending: police officers and firemen, hospitals and their staff physicians, monitors and repairmen for public utility services. For these workers, along with other "night-shift" workers, the problem of temporal coordination creates a kind of dilemma: either they must have a minimal relationship with their families and with other "normally" timed activities, or their families will be off-phase with the standard patterns of the community.[8] These problems on the small scale, statistically speaking, precisely indicate the barriers to "a flattening out" of the peaks and hollows in the use of urban space and capital resources. The attempt to reduce rush-hour traffic congestion by "staggered" daily work schedules has early limits if the worker is to have some time synchronized with other members of the family, and a staggered workweek would affect not only the family but also a host of associations ranging from churches to recreational groups.

The early Soviet attempt at a widely staggered workweek seems to have been aimed positively at a more constant use of capital and negatively at the church and family. The continuous workweek was introduced in 1929.[9] All enterprises and offices stayed open daily without a general day of rest. Workers had every fifth day off, so that one fifth of the employees were nominally absent on any given day. Higher officials often could not take their regular days off, and the daily shift in absentees created considerable chaos in banks, schools, and administrative offices. Families rarely enjoyed the same rest day for all members. On grounds that the shifting five-day schedule encouraged irresponsibility with respect to jobs and equipment, Stalin in 1931 decreed a change to a six-day week with a common rest day. In 1940 the seven-day week was restored, with Sunday the rest day and thus available for Christian religious observances, for these churches had not abandoned the old calendar. Even a revolutionary society requires some measure of temporal coordination out of working hours.

It is possible to imagine an entire society divided into, say, seven segments, each an exact cross section of all other forms of specialization and each following its own rhythm of activities. The coordination and the integrated and collective action essential to a viable system would, however, be extremely complicated and, indeed, hard to realize. The large city provides perhaps the closest approximation, and its rhythm remains remarkably uneven.

Planning and Temporal Discontinuities

In rare instances cities, such as Brasilia, the capital of Brazil, may be planned from their inception. The rather uniform evidence indicates that such plans are incomplete over the short run and notably fail to predict the future over the long run. For the vast majority of cities that have evolved without any plan or control until the last few decades, when zoning codes and planning commissions were introduced,[10] the sequence of development provides a multitude of illustrations of leads and lags.

Off-Phase Problem Solving

Although cities existed in the ancient world and subsist in the nonindustrial world today,[11] in the absence of a substantial agricultural surplus the preindustrial city was limited in population size and often included a measure of food production within its boundaries. Size was also limited by the transportation problem of providing daily or at least frequent supplies. Transportation, in fact, has been a major factor in the growth of cities in numbers and in individual size and an important element in shaping the ecological structure of metropolitan areas. Railroads, electrified street cars, and buses have affected the limits of the residential areas of cities, and subways, and other forms of rapid transit have facilitated movement within the city proper. The use of private automobiles has trended to extend the boundaries of commutation and particularly to divorce residence from proximity to fixed transportation routes. Yet the space requirements in the city for rail lines and terminals are small compared with the roadway and parking requirements for private cars, each carrying perhaps one or two passengers to and from work. As a means of handling this massive flow of traffic, city officials proceed to build expressways at tremendous cost per mile, in view of the expense of property condemnation and the preparation of submerged or elevated roadways to avoid "local" surface traffic. In virtually every instance such transportation developments are "tardy" with regard to traffic density, and the new routes often seem outdated or inadequate as soon as they are completed.

Off-phase problem solving seems indeed to be the recurrent theme running through most aspects of adaptation to urban change, and planning in general has been tardy, incomplete, inaccurate, and poorly enforced. With the superior wisdom of hindsight, it is now clear that the failure to extend and modernize public systems of rapid transit sets off a long chain of changes and conditions: traffic congestion, which may be intensified in some areas as it is alleviated in others by superhighways; the development of suburban shopping centers offering advantages in accessibility by private car as well as nearby parking space; circumferential highways designed to relieve downtown congestion by eliminating "through traffic" but also permitting easier communication between suburbs and thus the possibility of specialized suburban retail establishments; urban decay as the combined effect of these transportation changes (as well as others) leading to various urban renewal programs designed to restore central cities as acceptable places of residence and profitable places of commerce.

The list of failures to anticipate problems or to take timely preventive action is indeed impressive.[12] Zoning codes are commonly adopted *after* a noisome factory has been established in a residential area or rising land values encourage a developer to build small "look-alike" houses on tiny plots adjacent to more stately homes or to build high-rise apartments without parking facilities in an area already congested with street traffic and parked cars. Unless the offending structures are acquired by public authorities under the principle of eminent domain, they remain as testaments to temporal error, since by the equally honorable principle forbidding retroactive legislation the land uses that antedate zoning regulations are simply "nonconforming." Open spaces and access to streams or other bodies of water may disappear before community interest is effectively asserted. Air and stream pollution may be far advanced before corrective action is taken.

The Uneven Pace of Change

The speed with which the character of land use and the location of activities can change within a city is impressive. The urban ecologist's concepts of "invasion and succession"[13] give some flavor to the rapid transition of a residential zone to a commercial one or to the changing economic and ethnic composition of a residential area that has been "invaded" by an "undesirable" activity, such as manufacturing, or "undesirable" neighbors, such as Negroes. The impact of such alterations in the pace and direction of change may be different for the individuals involved and for the structure of the community as a whole, but for neither is it likely to be irrelevant or without strain.

Some other temporal discontinuities in city development are worthy of note, and not all of these appear to be capable of prevention even by exceptionally foresighted decision makers. The age structures of urban population, for example, are a product of general and differential fertility rates of the past and patterns of selective migration across unguarded city boundaries. The large decline of the birth rate during the Great Depression of the 1930's was especially sharp among urban populations, and school facilities and teachers came to be in excess supply. The pronounced birth-rate recovery during and after World War II was again sharpest among those urban populations in which it had been lowest, and city schools and the supply of teachers have become inadequate.

For many suburban communities the problems of timing of school construction can be projected into the future, but the forecast contains no clear indication of the action that could be taken to "even out" the phasing of construction. Many new suburban communities consist almost exclusively of young adults and their immature children. These homeowners (with mortgages) are precisely representative of current trends involving somewhat larger families rapidly produced, so that school construction represents a major part of community needs and tax-supported budgets. Without substantial residential mobility in the future, these homeowners and their children will grow inexorably older, and, after the foreseeable high schools and, possibly, community colleges have been built and staffed, what then? It would require an extensive rate of outmigration by parents as their children leave each stage of the school system and of inmigration of parents with children ready for that stage, or a marked extension of the number of children and period of childbearing in most families, to avoid a rather substantial oversupply of school facilities only a decade or so from now.

Some other forms of construction for community services

seem to have a kind of inherent but infrequent recurrence of crisis. The supply of potable water for many larger cities requires costly construction of aqueducts or purification plants, which then cannot be added to in small and steady increments but must have new major construction to increase the supply for an ensuing period (usually shorter than predicted by the plan). Sewage disposal often represents the same kind of discontinuity in construction. For some other services, such as light, power, and telephone, small and frequent additions to capacity may be feasible over considerable periods, though even these may reach limits that can be extended only by major construction of new facilities.

Privately owned utility companies in the United States, and perhaps publicly owned facilities also, indeed seem to operate with an excessively short-run planning horizon. The essential ingredients for predicting demand levels are population forecasts multiplied by predicted trends in per capita use. Since digging up the streets to lay new pipes and cables is an expensive process, economic wisdom would seem to encourage installing the carrying capacity, currently in excess, for as long a period as reasonable prediction permits—limited, of course, by current capital resources for investments with delayed returns. Capital supplies, in fact, may be the limiting factor, though poor planning cannot be eliminated as a strong possibility. The rates of utility companies are generally regulated in terms of return on investment, and the companies may therefore be less able than many corporations to finance expansion out of retained earnings not distributed to stockholders. The frequency with which streets are torn up for additional installations, thus substantially adding to the congestion of surface traffic, suggests that the suppliers are "too closely" on-phase with increases in use.

"Excessive" Urbanization

The extremely rapid urbanization of the principal cities in the economically underdeveloped countries [14] presents problems of temporal phasing that exceed in magnitude those faced by most cities of the industrialized countries. The causes of the rapid urban migration are, as usual, a mixture of the "push" of deteriorating conditions in rural areas and the "pull" of the real or fancied advantages of the cities, including the association of their typical forms of economic activity with the rapid spread of "rising aspirations" that is such a prominent feature of the contemporary world. Whatever the causes, the consequences include an expansion of urban populations more rapid than that of regular employment opportunities and thus a concentration of poverty and various indicators of social disorganization. From a community viewpoint, the rate of growth exceeds the supply of houses, streets, potable water, sewage facilities, light and power, and public transportation. The perimeter of the old city is not a residential area for well-to-do commuters but a noisome suburban slum. The visible presence of these conditions and their implications for political disorder—it is often the national capitals that are growing most rapidly—affect the timetable of allocation of resources for national economic planning, for investments in urban public services would not otherwise stand high in the priority scale for economic development. Plans, both at the national and community levels, are thus disrupted by an excessively rapid urbanization, which could be prevented only by the imposition of a degree of political control inconsistent with democratic institutions and probably inconsistent with the effective maintenance of power by presently constituted governments. One can imagine, for example, the furor that would be created if the government of a newly independent African state attempted to institute "pass laws" as a way of preventing internal migration. Planners may be forced to a greater geographical decentralization of development measures, including health facilities and schools as well as improved employment opportunities, than would be "ideal" in terms of the advantages of centralization and the concentration of people and facilities that cities afford.

Urban planning and the control of community structure are everywhere impeded by another kind of political consideration —the forms of local government and the geographical limits of their application. Since the days of the walled cities, and even they outgrew their boundaries centuries ago, the aggregation of people in urban places has shown slight regard for maps and arbitrary boundaries. Not only do local officeholders represent "vested interests" unfavorable to governmental structures that coincide with the functional areas of communities, but if some supergovernments such as various "metropolitan authorities" are painfully established they must either represent duplicative structures or attempt to secure cooperation and compromise among the archaic and anachronistic organizations.[15] Planning for the extended community under these circumstances is likely to be a fairly ineffectual "academic" operation unless the plans include procedures for political implementation. The dilemma posed by urban growth everywhere is that local political autonomy is somewhat threatened by a truly metropolitan government, yet uncoordinated local control increases the prospects for chaotic uses of space and improvident uses of time.

NOTES

1. Amos H. Hawley, *Human Ecology* (New York: Ronald Press, 1950), Chapter 12, "Community Structure," especially pp. 223–232.
2. *Ibid.*, Chapter 15, "Temporal Aspect of Ecological Organization."
3. *Ibid.*, p. 306.
4. *Ibid.*, p. 305.
5. See especially Gerald William Breese, *The Daytime Population of the Central Business District of Chicago* (Chicago: University of Chicago Press, 1940).
6. *Ibid.*, pp. 174–180.
7. Hawley, *op. cit.*, pp. 311–312.
8. This point has been made with regard to "time and the railroader" by W. Fred Cottrell, *The Railroader* (Stanford: Stanford University Press, 1940), pp. 71–74.
9. This summary is based on Leonard E. Hubbard, *Soviet Labor and Industry* (London: Macmillan, 1942), pp. 47, 59, 98.
10. The ideas of planning and zoning are quite old, but the first comprehensive zoning ordinance in the United States was passed by New York City in 1916, and the first planning commission in the United States with power to establish a master plan was provided for in the 1918 City Charter of Cincinnati. In Britain comprehensive planning is usually

dated as starting with the Housing, Town Planning, etc. Act of 1909. See Beverly J. Pooley, *Planning and Zoning in the United States* (Ann Arbor: University of Michigan Press, 1957), p. 42; Arthur B. Gallion, *The Urban Pattern* (New York: Van Nostrand, 1950), pp. 226–229; Edward A. Bassett, *The Master Plan* (New York: Russell Sage Foundation, 1938, pp. 74–79; William Ashworth, *The Genesis of Modern British Town Planning* (London: Routledge & Kegan Paul, 1954).

11. See, for example, Gideon Sjoberg, *The Preindustrial City* (Glencoe, Ill.: Free Press, 1960).

12. For a discussion of the importance, but small use, of long-range planning, see John W. Dykeman, "Of Time and the Plan," *J. Amer. Inst. Planners,* **28**, 141–143, May 1962.

13. See Hawley, *op. cit.*, pp. 400–402.

14. See Philip M. Hauser, ed., *Urbanization in Asia and the Far East* (Calcutta: UNESCO Research Centre, 1957); Hauser, ed., *Urbanization in Latin America* (New York: Columbia University Press, 1961; International Afrcian Institute, *Social Implications of Industrialization and Urbanization in Africa South of the Sahara* (Paris: UNESCO, 1956).

15. See Jean Gottmann, *Megalopolis* (New York: Twentieth Century Fund, 1961), especially Chapter 14, "Sharing a Partitioned Land"; Robert C. Wood, *1400 Governments* (Cambridge: Harvard University Press, 1961); Edward C. Banfield and Morton Grodzins, *Government and Housing in Metropolitan Areas* (New York: McGraw-Hill, 1958).

Eight

The Economy

Economic growth has become a major concern of all people everywhere or at least of their statesmen and political spokesmen. Time is a prominent component in the quest for growth: in the attempts to speed the rate of change and in the manifold problems of synchronization and sequence that rapid growth entails. The anxiety of the governments of the economically underdeveloped countries to secure rapid increases in production immediately, and hopefully to "catch up" with the living standards (and perhaps military power) of the advanced countries in "the future," is shared in a somewhat altered form in the leading industrial countries. The Soviet Union seeks, at various specific future dates, to equal the output and income of the United States, whereas American political leaders and their economic advisers express concern that the Soviet Union may do just that because their political system permits a higher rate of savings and investment and thus a more rapid rate of potential economic expansion.

The relatively slow evolutionary processes of economic change —deriving from essentially accidental innovations in the technology of production, transportation, or storage, from the imposition of stable political administration over larger areas, or from the discovery of new territories and resources—still occur, but they appear minor compared with the vast energies devoted to deliberate change and to the planning and control of sequences and rates. For deliberate change, time becomes a specific variable as well as a limiting condition, a matter for calculation and control, not simply a period or era to be recorded retrospectively. The speed of change and the attempt to direct and control both sequence and rate add to rather than reduce the problems of synchronization and balance and the value that time takes on as a wasting resource.

A national economy is something more than a business enterprise or a local market writ large. The magnitude and diversity of activities involved in the production and distribution of goods and services for an entire society present special problems of coordination. Some of these large-scale economic problems are primarily questions of control, but each has one or more temporal dimensions also. The regulatory system encompassing competitive economic activities, for example, is almost certain to be off-phase, since procedural innovations in competitive strategies are extremely likely and their disallowance or control will be in some measure "tardy." [1] Similarly, the political elements in the organization of production, both within the enterprise and in the form of "combinations of restraint of trade," are likely to exhibit various leads and lags with respect to strategies and their regulation. The aggregative and collective effects of economic activity, for the short term and the long, display a wondrous variety of problems of synchronization and sequence, of discordant phasing of rates of change.

Inventories of Economic Time

Since "man does not live by bread alone," the economy is always an aspect of society, and an essential one, but it is never a total social system. No society, however poor in the aggregate or however precarious the sustenance of its individual members, could endure without political order, codes of conduct, common cognitive and normative orientations, effective socialization of the young, and so on. It is the establishment and extension of the market as a mechanism for allocation and exchange of services—and that is characteristic of relatively prosperous societies—that provides a pronounced economic tint to all sorts of social activities. Money then becomes wondrously useful not only for homely necessities and gaudy luxuries but also for travel, the enjoyment of the arts, and the indulgence of philanthropic impulses. It is a mistake to equate the utility of money with "materialism," for in the nature of the case the poor are likely to be more materialistic than the rich.

The Labor Force as the Supply of Time

The part of a society that can be said to constitute the economy, and thus the "size" of the economic system, is difficult to compare across substantial differences in institutions. In the absence of something like a market mechanism, which gives a measurable "economic value" to goods and services, the activities that yield "production" and involve "labor" can hardly be distinguished among the great variety of socially useful acts.[2] And, we have just noted, with such a market mechanism many services having nothing to do with physical sustenance of material goods come to have a measurable economic value. The latter situation at least provides an "operational test" of the aggregate of economic time. It is the time that is financially rewarded, whatever the function performed.

Wherever a market system permits an approximate distinction between the activities that constitute "labor" and those that do not, the concept of the "labor force" is appropriate. As conventionally used, the "labor force" consists of those who are in the labor market, whether employed by others or working on their own account, and includes those not actually at work but seeking work, temporarily laid off, on sick leave, on vacation, and so on.[3] When the labor force so defined is multiplied by the number of hours of, say a standard workweek, the result is an approximation to the economic time inventory for that period; the aggregate hours actually worked would provide a more precise measure of total time use in the economy, the difference constituting a kind of measure of time waste.

The size of the labor force itself is a product of many factors, some of which, in a complex world, are themselves interrelated. The maximum size of the labor force is comprised of all persons capable of any activity sufficiently useful to command an economic reward. The actual size will be that total minus various subtractions.[4] The total population, like that portion of it "old enough" and "young enough" to work, is a demographic fact —the consequence of past births, eroded by deaths, plus or minus the net flow of migration. The actual labor force is influenced in size, and in its age-sex composition, by those demographic phenomena but not precisely determined by them. Minimum and maximum working ages are fixed by law and custom. Similarly, the participation of women in directly compensated labor (and thus excluding housewives not otherwise employed) is strongly affected by institutional and market forces. Some persons otherwise able to work may be exempted because their private wealth makes gainful employment unnecessary. Some persons who are below the minimum physical, mental, or educational levels of employability may be potentially willing and indeed eager to work.

These levels and indeed other factors affecting labor force participation are subject to some variation according to the state of "demand" for labor (including politically determined demand for military or other "public" or emergency service). A shortage of labor may, by market principles, raise wages and thus induce those not previously in the labor market to seek employment. Poor employment prospects may not only force some persons such as housewives out of the labor force but also may encourage the young to postpone the quest for employment, perhaps by seeking additional education.

Thus "labor-force-participation rates" for various age-sex categories are likely to vary from time to time and between economies, and the same variability applies to other social categories.

Various nonparticipating or exempt groups plus the unemployed at any time constitute essentially unused "reserves" of economic time, subject to possible use if the general level of employment or particular emergencies indicate a closer approximation to the maximum than is the normal situation.

Impediments to Interchangeable Units

The economy exhibits on a large scale what the administrative organization shows on a more limited base: the limited interchangeability of man-hour units because of differences in occupational qualifications. An economy at any time may accordingly have simultaneous surpluses and shortages of labor, and a complex and changeful industrial economy will almost certainly have them at all times.

Some small part of the failure to match supply and demand may be owing to unemployed workers' ignorance of opportunities elsewhere, to the financial and psychological costs of changing residences, and possibly even to changing to a different industry or sector of the economy. A highly centralized or totalitarian economic system, by coordination of labor information and the bald imposition of administrative power, may have less "frictional" waste of labor time than more open and individualistic systems.

Most of the barriers to mobility, however, are more intrinsic: the unemployed or underemployed worker simply lacks the qualifications for the positions that are open. The occupational composition of the labor force at any time reflects past temporal allocations to education, formal and otherwise, and perfect educational planning for an uncertain future exists nowhere. "Technological unemployment" would be eliminated by either of two unrealistic sets of conditions: (1) the rate of technological change and of economic expansion would be such that all new occupations would be filled by new entrants to the labor force, whereas the demand for obsolescent occupations would decrease in exact proportion to the rate of retirement of those currently practicing them; (2) the "automatic" correctives to technological displacement through lower prices and consequent diversion of demand to new products, or higher profits and consequent new investments and associated labor demand, would provide jobs with appropriate levels and varieties of skills, precisely for the displaced workers.

Both of these compensating mechanisms operate in some degree but with many "frictions." One important category of frictions is represented by wasted economic time in the form of unemployment. Another represents the training time necessary for a displaced worker to reach any skill level and variety adequate to secure employment, which may still have lower financial rewards than the position from which he was displaced.

Although economic time inventories clearly have finite limits if other essential or valued time commitments are to endure, most economies operate well below them. The underemployment characteristic of most poor countries and regions mainly reflects a shortage of capital and often of managerial skills. The unemployed worker in advanced countries exhibits a failure of the economy to provide "immediate" adjustment to rapid change. Individual readjustment can be facilitated before entering the labor force by a type of education that emphasizes the continuous capacity to learn rather than the acquisition of a narrowly defined vocational skill. The changes in occupational demand attendant on technological and market changes may also encourage the development of programs of adult vocational retraining. The inventories of economic time, in sum, are not meaningful in the aggregate but only in their appropriate distributions by type and quality. To keep that quality appropriate and current requires, paradoxically, additional or relocated inputs of time in teaching and learning.

Interdependence and Coordination

The size of any social system is a necessary but not sufficient condition for internal specialization of activities—of occupations and products in the economy, of activities and organizations within a religious denomination, and of agencies and services in the structure of the state. Specialization also requires ways of making the consequent interdependence effective: at a minimum, effective communication and a common body of rules of procedure. For specialization in the production of goods, transportation of raw materials and semifinished products is likely to be necessary, and at the very least a system of distribution linking the specialized producer and the generalized consumer is essential.

The other side of specialization is coordination, and there are two classic ways of achieving it: a system of reciprocity or exchange and a system providing for subjection to a common "administrative" authority. In all modern economies these two forms of coordination are intermixed, and the intermixture is further complicated by a major extension of a simple principle: any system of coordination will depend for its continuity on a moral order, that is, a body of rules of conduct, applicable to participants in exchange as well as, obviously, to participants in organized units. The major extension of this principle is the prominent role of the state in modern economies, not just as rulemaker and rule enforcer but also as producer and consumer, tax collector and distributor of benefits, the producer of money and the regulator of its supply, the determiner or supporter of prices, and, in varying degrees, the locus of decision on what is to be produced and in what amounts. In the capitalist economies the role of the state is partly indirect, operating through the market, but also direct, as in administrative regulation of conditions of employment, the content of food and drug products, or the disclosure of information to investors.

Temporal Dimensions of Coordination

All forms of coordination involve problems of time, synchronization, and sequence. In the indirect and impersonal market, since production and distribution are not instantaneous, the producer and trader must estimate the time lag for goods to reach the market and the state of "demand" at that time. In a fractionated and competitive market each decision maker must make his estimates independently (or the market loses a major competitive feature) but must take into account guesses regarding the behavior of his competitors, including their timetables. Thus, if a producer predicts an expanding market but has some reason to suppose that his competitors have a head start in increasing production, he must either try to make up time or rely on some differentiating strategy in order to get some "share" of the sales. Even if goods are in short supply and a "seller's market" prevails, delays in production or distribution may result in the physical waste of perishable goods or financial costs for storage and transportation. Time, then, is a major factor in economic efficiency, and timing is a major factor in competitive success. Products that reach the market "too soon" at the very least tie up capital in inventory; those that reach the market "too late" will result in partial or total waste. It is therefore understandable that market-forecasting services are sold to business enterprisers and that occasionally the consumer, particularly the prospective purchaser of some "discretionary" item, will attempt to time his purchases to get the most favorable terms.

In relatively "pure" markets, that is, those with large numbers of independent buyers and sellers, errors of timing may have little or no aggregative effects. Some businesses may fail and others gain in relative economic position, with only comparatively minor effects on the supply and prices of goods and services. Even with large numbers of participants, however, independence of action may be impaired by imitation rather than by combination or collusion. Thus the relative volatility of stock markets is in considerable measure the result of a kind of "self-fulfilling prophecy." [5] The prediction of a decline leads to sales that bring on the decline, which induces larger numbers to sell and hasten the fall in prices. A reverse process, though usually slower, can be created by self-confirming optimism. Clever traders can make profits either by being ahead of the trend or otherwise off-phase—in the simplest buying terms, buying on the down-swing and selling on the rise.

Almost-clever traders can also lose fortunes by slight errors of estimate in the timing of changes in trend and their duration.

When large administrative units operate in a market, the "purity" of competition is likely to be impaired, and the errors of coordination and timing have more far-reaching effects. For example, large investments in new plant capacity may be ready for productive return when the market has "turned soft," or an unpredicted upturn in the market may result in shortages and higher prices which cannot be quickly rectified because of the lead time required for new productive capacity. A common but independent response to a shortage by several large producers may result once more in excess capacity, and a kind of self-confirming cycle of surplus and shortage occurs. When productive capacity must be constructed in large and relatively discontinuous increments— not an additional machine but an additional plant equipped with interrelated machines—some leads and lags are virtually inevitable.

A major portion of governmental influence on the economy is directed toward "dampening" the extremes of oscillation, correcting "lags," and breaking "bottlenecks" that impede the growth of many other functionally dependent sectors of the economy. Thus even in the traditional laissez-faire economies transportation and communication, power, banking, and education have been the objects of governmental action or assistance. These elements of "social overhead capital" are highly strategic both functionally and temporally, for without them other forms of production and coordination would be seriously or totally inhibited.

Independent decisions in timing, we have noted, may lead to cumulative as well as compensatory trends and errors in estimate. Direct administrative controls or indirect governmental measures, such as the manipulation of the interest rate through the central bank or the changing of tax rates, always have a mixed impact on various sectors of the economy. Centralized policies affecting the whole economy are at least as subject to error as more decentralized and partial policies, and the administrative complexity of policy formulation and implementation is likely to reduce the possibility of speedy and short-range alterations.

Questions of Speed and Flexibility

The speed with which changes can be made in economic arrangements merits some additional comments. It is axiomatic that a high degree of interdependence, even if the system is centrally administered, does not adapt easily and speedily to major alterations. This principle applies even to mechanical specialization. A truly automated production of, say, refrigerators requires such a specialized and intricate network of mechanical installations and controlled sequence of operations that even a change of design may be a slow and expensive process. Though certain technological efforts have been directed precisely to the development of functionally flexible machines, extreme mechanical specialization appears to be more common. A substantial alteration in the demand for products will thus be more costly in time and money than would be the case for a less highly "developed" technology of production. Extreme individual and organizational specialization has precisely the same kind of implications.

Now, modern economies are highly specialized and interdependent, yet marked by rapid change: in products and services, in technology of production and techniques of administration, in markets and market prices, and in the range and specifications of occupations. The explanations of this situation are several and interrelated. Although the older "liberal" economies are specialized, their integration is actually rather loose; they afford extensive opportunities for innovation, for the operation of competitive strategies, for diversity of markets and occupations, and for mobility. Many economic changes are, at least initially, additions to the technology or products or services rather than outright substitutions. Because time and money are scarce, novelties must compete with standard procedures and products and may in fact actually displace some of them. Size, however, does permit diversity as well as coordinated specialization, and new elements may simply find a place while old ones persist. To take a simple but significant example, the alternative ways of manufacturing a fairly standard product, say pig iron, may represent different technical processes, the inventions of which bracket a period of fifty years. The least efficient procedures may eventually disappear if the competition becomes rigorous, but the fact that the older investments have long since been amortized may permit the "outdated" technology to survive.

The other side of the picture of the relation between interdependence and rate of change should also be noted. The impressive rates of economic growth achieved by the centralized control of the Soviet Union are based on a relatively narrow and rather stringently controlled range of goods and services, administrative procedures, types of occupations, avenues of mobility, and so on. Even if diversity were not severely restricted for ideological reasons and for reasons of concentration of efforts on a limited range of goals, it is doubtful that such an "integrated" economic and social system would permit change of the magnitude and range evident in pluralistic societies. The deliberate character of many changes in industrial societies is not inconsistent with a great many potential innovators and a great many contexts of innovation. Administrative coordination is likely to increase the resources available for particular innovations and to impede both the range of other innovations and the importance of chance or accidental discovery.

Fluctuations and Temporal Phasing

A prominent feature of capitalist economies over the last century and a half has been the "business cycle," or, since the regularity and clarity of changes in economic magnitudes is in considerable doubt, the more contemporary concept of "economic fluctuations." [6] An explanation of such fluctuations is by no means agreed on by economists and is not explored here. Certain partial self-confirming cycles deriving from independent but parallel or imitative actions have been noted in preceding paragraphs. Complications develop, however, in part because not all phases of complex economic systems move "synchronously" and in part because some long-term trends and fluctuations such as net rate of savings [7] or birth rates may have rather fundamental but subtle effects.

Prosperity and Depression

For perhaps a century, ending with the Great Depression of the 1930's, the Marxian prophecy of successive periodic crises of ever-increasing intensity seemed to be confirmed. The greater intensity was largely an indication of functional interdependence within and between economic systems so that a decline of some phase of economic activity tended to become "contagious." The contemporary confidence of most economists and experts in economic policy that depressions of comparable severity will not recur rests on the use of a rather wide battery of governmental measures designed to restrain extremes, *to insulate and fragment depressed economic sectors,* and thus to make possible timely corrective measures. The continued recurrence of "recessions," though the temporal period is relatively short (since around 1950), gives some support to the optimistic view and at the same time indicates that the controls are neither perfect nor always correctly timed when viewed retrospectively. Insurance and quasi-insurance measures, such as unemployment benefits, attempt to cushion the impact of adversity by spreading risks both cross-sectionally and temporally (saving in "good times" for support in "hard times").

Births and Deaths

Trends in population growth in both historical and contemporary terms provide some additional dimensions to long-term temporal phasing. The historic trend in birth and death rates associated with industrialization was rather uniformly marked by a decline in death rates a good many years before the decline in birth rates, with resulting rapid population growth.[8] The dire Malthusian predictions of increasing misery were not, in fact, confirmed, as the settlement of new territories and development of new production generally exceeded the pace of population increase. Since a growing population adds producers, and consumers, if employed, create an expanding market, the general effect of this growth may well have been economically favorable.[9] Under far less favorable circumstances the same optimism is, of course, inappropriate to densely settled and poor countries today. But in the United States and Western Europe the recovery of the birth rate since World War II is generally regarded as favorable to both labor supplies and consumer demand.

With the widespread availability and use of contraception in Western countries, temporal variations in birth rates appear to be closely linked to various economic indicators, including, especially, levels of employment. Now this suggests the possibility, for which there is already some evidence,[10] of a moderately long-term, self-confirming, but "perennially" off-phase cycle. The argument goes that the period of full employment following World War II was partly a consequence of labor shortages resulting from the maturity of small birth cohorts born during the Great Depression. The high birth rates of the exceptionally prosperous period may yield excess labor supplies by the late 1960's, with consequent unemployment and reduced birth rates, and so on. In other words, because of the intrinsic time lag in reaching maturity, variations in labor supplies may be keyed to situations two decades earlier than to current economic factors.

The time lag between decline in death rates and the acceptance and practice of the idea of rational control of fertility presents a serious strain on the efforts of underdeveloped areas to achieve a rapid increase in per capita income. Rapid population growth diverts limited resources from capital expansion to current consumption, and high birth rates have an especially adverse effect on the expansion of general education. Thus positive efforts are being made in some countries (for example, India and Pakistan) to reduce birth rates more rapidly than they fell in the older industrial countries.

The Sequence of Modernization

Speed, in fact, is sought in a wide range of social transformations in the developing countries. The existence of modern technology of all sorts, the products of that technology, and even of alternative models for achieving industrialization mean that the currently underdeveloped countries need not replicate either the sequence or the rate of change experienced in the West.[11] Antibiotics may be adopted before aspirin, electric or atomic furnaces for smelting ore may make coking coal unnecessary, and centralized planning and control may obviate the uncertain course of private investment decisions.

There are, of course, some limits to the simple selective adoption of products and processes, administrative devices, and forms of organization. The use of the most advanced productive technology requires a certain functional context: trained operators, maintenance men, and repair parts. Similarly, certain contemporary theories of administration, involving decentralization and widespread participation in operating decisions, assume a highly educated and experienced labor force.

The attempt to compress time, to jump a period of decades or a century, may be exceptionally costly or in some instances impossible. The most advanced productive technology is likely to be capital-intensive but labor saving. Yet capital is acutely scarce and labor is generally abundant in underdeveloped areas. For nationalistic reasons political leaders may insist on ultramodern plants, whereas cheaper and more labor-intensive installations would appear to be the economically rational course.

For limited purposes, time indeed can be bought or borrowed by importing capital, technology, and certain strategic kinds of administrative and technical skills. But the resources of the advanced countries are simply not adequate to "modernize" the economies of two thirds of the world's population in the course of a few years. Local resources, material and human, local savings and investments, and local administration and distribution must in the nature of the case supply a major portion of the ingredients of economic growth. To improve the quality and use of these ingredients will require time—not necessarily in centuries but certainly in decades.

Human resources are likely to provide the most intractably delaying ingredients of change (as well as, of course, the source and beneficiaries of change). Physiological maturation and the acquisition of educated skills are time-consuming processes. References to "Stone Age cultures" in journalistic discussions of the underdeveloped world are generally inappropriate and always misleading, for the implication is that they are separated from advanced societies by millennia. No area of the world is going to evolve in its own slow and isolated fashion, but as a part of a world that is in many respects a single system, though politically divided and economically diversified. There is simply no evidence that "backwardness" is biological, and the rate of cultural change is limited only by the resources directed to that goal and the time required to acquire new knowledge and skills, new values and habits of thought, new norms of conduct, and the internalized conviction that they are "right." The speed with which the "doctrine of economic development" has spread to all areas of the world, at least among political leaders, belies the notion that values are intrinsically slow to change. Yet the costs of change, including the sacrifice of cherished institutions inconsistent with a modernized economy, are not trivial and will certainly cause strains and delays and possible failures. Men may simultaneously foster change and regret and resist its consequences. Anachronisms abound in the modern world and are likely to do so in the foreseeable future, but that is mainly because some clocks are speeding up, not because others are slowing down or not running at all.

NOTES

1. See Wilbert E. Moore, *Social Change* (Englewood Cliffs: Prentice-Hall, forthcoming), Chapter III, "Small-Scale Changes."

2. See Wilbert E. Moore, "The Exportability of the Labor Force Concept," *Amer. Sociolog. Rev.*, 18, 68–72, February 1953.

3. See A. J. Jaffe and Charles D. Stewart, *Manpower Resources and Utilization* (New York: Wiley, 1951).

4. See Wilbert E. Moore, *Industrial Relations and the Social Order*, rev. ed. (New York: Macmillan, 1951), Chapters XIX and XX.

5. See Robert K. Merton, *Social Theory and Social Structure*, rev. ed. (Glencoe, Ill.: Free Press, 1957), Chapter 11, "The Self-Fulfilling Prophecy."

6. See, for example, Paul A. Samuelson, *Economics*, 4th ed. (New York: McGraw-Hill, 1958), Part II, "Determination of National Income and Its Fluctuations," especially Chapter 13, "Business Cycles and Forecasting."

7. See Simon Kuznets, *Quantitative Aspects of the Economic Growth of Nations. 1: Levels and Variability of Rates of Growth*, published as supplement to Vol. 5, October 1956 issue of *Economic Development and Cultural Change*.

8. See Wilbert E. Moore, "Industrialization and Social Change," in Bert F. Hoselitz and Wilbert E. Moore, eds., *Industrialization and Society* (The Hague: Mouton, 1962), Chapter 15, especially pp. 381–383.

9. See Simon Kuznets, "Population Change and Aggregate Output," in National Bureau of Economic Research, *Demographic and Economic Change in Developed Countries* (Princeton: Princeton University Press, 1960), pp. 324–340.

10. See Frank W. Notestein, "Mortality, Fertility, the Size-Age Distribution, and the Growth Rate," *ibid.*, pp. 261–275; the off-phase cycle is suggested by John V. Grauman in his "Comment" on Notestein's paper, pp. 275–282.

11. See Wilbert E. Moore, "Industrialization and Social Change."

$\mathcal{N}ine$

The World and Universe

The view of the earth as a speck in the seemingly infinite reaches of space, which numbers untold billions of stellar bodies, and of man's history as a bare instant in the infinite reaches of time is sobering to man's arrogance and to his anthropocentric view of the universe. Yet such a deflating cosmological view is scarcely part of ordinary human experience, and it is hardly surprising that most of man's preoccupations are bounded by finite space and all-too-limited time.

One has only to look at the pace of social change, from man's physical inventions that have served his adaptation to and major mastery of his environment to the wondrous variety of organizations and physical objects, of esthetic forms and religious beliefs, of amusements and verifiable information, to understand that *social* time operates on a clock that is constantly accelerating. Not all of that acceleration is encouraging, either to man's capacity for a tolerable degree of control of his social arrangements or to his capacity for physical survival, which, for an inherently social creature, still means social survival.

In concluding our exploration of the ways in which the limits and flows of time intersect with man's social life, we shall look briefly at the temporal order exhibited in the realm of national states and then make some sketches on the largest canvas of all, the relation of man to time in his world and universe.

The State and Its Temporal Claims

In almost every area of the world national states, or nationalistic political activity in dependent territories, have an impact on ordinary personal and social life for which the Nineteenth Century provided virtually no precedent. Greece and Rome and some Oriental empires supply examples of highly political social orders. Indeed strong, centralized, and pervasive rule occurred frequently in the ancient world and even in the premodern period in parts of Africa and the New World. The spread of political participation in the democratic states of the last century did not mean a correlative influence of the state in ordinary life; on the contrary. Many of the monarchical and dictatorial regimes represented a thin urban layer over a peasantry that was essentially politically inert.

The world wars of the Twentieth Century and the appearance and persistence of profound conflict in political ideology have affected entire populations in the more powerful nations and in many others as well. The dual revolution of economic modernization and nationalistic independence in economically underdeveloped and politically dependent areas has spread the pervasive influence of political concerns into most inhabited sectors of the globe.

It is really pointless to ask whether the speed of social transformation in the contemporary world is "primarily" ideological, economic, or political in source, for the three are inextricably intermeshed. Where one or another element seems to lead the pace of change or to dominate the course of transition, the others will be found in close temporal and functional proximity. The polity, however, will either be the instrumentality of change or the recipient of its tensions and problems.

An unmolested state without internal or external ambitions might regard time as critical only for the rare occurrence of urgent internal problems and otherwise as an orderly unfolding of history, marked by relatively insignificant political succession and little else. Such states in the past have encouraged historians to collapse decades or centuries into a period or era, quickly summarized. But, for the modern state, both the present and future are marked with hazards and changing aspirations, and time figures largely as an element of policy.

Political claims on time tend to be residual or fairly limited, even in totalitarian states. As a specialized structure, the state and its organizational apparatus represents an administrative organization for its employees and a kind of "involuntary association," but one with limited appeals and demands, for the ordinary citizen.

In fact, in pluralistic democracies "normal" political participation is voluntary, and part of it may offer options such as contending parties. Elections in these countries are rarely compulsory, and in any event not time consuming, and office seeking and office holding are optional.

The law, it is true, is more ubiquitous and demanding than politics. Yet the law is generally a codification and specialization of the normative system, and compliance with it is not precisely political in character. Only those laws that relate to the affairs of government or to special regulations—such as filing tax returns, securing permits and licenses, or having vehicles inspected—could be said to require identifiable time commitments. The positive obligations of the citizen with regard to law enforcement, other than his own compliance, are neither great nor clearly defined, for enforcement tends to be reserved to public employees. Jury service, though nominally compulsory, is usually determined by a combination of selectivity and chance, and evasion, at least in the United States, is relatively easy. (It follows that juries are, in fact, disproportionately drawn from sectors of the population that have more discretionary time than the ordinary full-time worker enjoys.)

In Communist and other totalitarian countries the state tends to pervade the social structure, which becomes, to employ a useful but ugly term, "politicized." Political considerations tend to "intrude" in familial, occupational, and even associational affairs, just as the economy tends to provide a market or financial aspect to other organizations in all modern economic systems. This pervasiveness of politics, of party loyalty, and "proper" ideological orientations may in a sense represent extreme temporal claims for the state, for little is politically irrelevant. Yet it appears more meaningful to regard politicization as providing a peculiar qualitative character to diverse social activities, which, however, do not necessarily become functionally political.

It is especially in military service or in the conscription of labor for various internal emergencies that states exert maximum temporal claims on their citizens. The state's claim may, in effect, be total, at least for the duration of the conflict, the emergency, or the period of "regular" military or public service. And it is only the state, in modern times, that can exact the death penalty for convicted offenders and require death in military operations as an incident of national policy. Now death does not add to the temporal inventories of states, but precisely depletes them. If war losses generally were translated into lost life expectancies, the cost in time would be impressive. A million deaths at an average age of 20 would cost the society a total of approximately fifty million man-years, assuming a normal expectation of life of seventy years. If time is indeed valuable, such irretrievable waste represents a prodigal expenditure, which may, of course, be viewed as justified in terms of the collective goals, which are, however, meaningfully applicable only to the living.

The Sense of History

The state, as the "residuary legatee of unsolved social problems," reacts to various strains and emergencies, as discussed in the preceding two chapters with regard to cities and the economy. Over the long term, the state, even in pluralistic societies, thus tends to accumulate functions. The state, to put it a little differently, becomes a principal agency of tension management [1] in societies that are intrinsically rife with tensions arising in part from un-equal rates of change. Inevitably, as the state reacts to problems of timing, of leads and lags, and directs part of the course of change on its own initiative, some of the problems with which it deals will be of its own making. The secondary and tertiary effects of any policy will rarely if ever be uniformly positive and wholly foreseen, so that the consequences of past political poli-cies provide part of the problems of the present.

Temporal Strategies

The national state combines the distinct functions of main-tenance of order internally and maintenance of relations with other states, including military action and defense. Timing is of extreme importance in military policy: in actual battle, by strik-ing first and unexpectedly, the enemy's capacity to resist or re-taliate may be impaired or destroyed; in peacetime "defense" new technology of weapons gives a temporary advantage to the innovator. Even in ordinary "diplomacy" timing is not inconse-quential, and contemporary great-power diplomacy is scarcely ordinary. American foreign policy, for example, becomes en-tangled with the military, economic, and social strategies of other countries. In the "cold war" the policies of allies ranging from military prepardness to the movements of gold "require" tem-poral coordination that is not always forthcoming. An appropriate international action may be delayed or be taken prematurely be-cause of the internal political situation in one country or another.

Temporal strategies also, and especially, apply to relations with "uncommitted" countries. The expectation of outside financial assistance has become part of the development plans in Asian, African, and Latin American countries, and providing this assist-ance, say by the United States, is justified in part by international political strategies, aimed at keeping the assisted countries friendly or at least neutral. As former colonies become independent states, speed in offering them aid has tended to make mere diplomatic recognition old-fashioned.

Continuity: The Past and Future

Over the longer term, continuity with the past is a major element in the claims of the state to legitimacy in its exercise of power. Even revolutionary governments will ordinarily attempt to find some elements of a traditional and valued past as part of the base on which it proposes to create a better future. The passion for innovation, for the creation of a social order radically different from the regime overthrown, does not remove all sense of historically continuity. The tradition may be ideological rather than structural: the liberal tradition of the "Enlightenment" for the French Revolution, the Marxist tradition for the Russian Revolution. Occasionally the distant past serves to offer material for restoration. Thus the land reform following the Mexican Revolution established the Ejido and thereby "restored" a pre-Columbian pattern of communal land ownership with, however, individual family allotments and cultivation.[2]

Many newly independent countries attempt to create a distinctive history especially to establish a link with a past interrupted by the "colonial interlude." Thus in Africa precolonial regimes are being refurbished, not to be restored but to lend strength to the claimed capacity for self-rule and to provide a distinctly African tradition not linked to the objectively more evident reality that the actual boundaries, the administrative structure of the government, the principal features of the economy, and the educational system were established by the colonial regime. Perhaps the most extreme case of seeking historial authentication of territorial boundaries as well as various elements of political ideology is the Biblical basis of legitimacy claimed by Israel. Mussolini, it will be recalled, had grand plans for restoration of the Roman Empire, and DeGaulle has dreams of glory for a militarily weak and politically fractionated France.

The past is useful not only as a traditional foundation for current legitimacy but also as a precedent for persistence into the indefinite future. The state attributes to itself immortality, and its leaders are expected to act in ways appropriate to ensure future survival and future welfare. Even in pluralistic societies there are strong elements of sanctification of the state, of viewing patriotism as a religious virtue, a matter of belief not subject to question.[3] Although in peacetime in pluralistic societies the actual government (but not the nation) may be treated as a partisan interest group, in wartime or periods of enduring ideological conflict and international political competition the state is viewed as a superindividual and enduring collectivity. For such an immortal state the past is assimilated to the present, a "living heritage," and citizens of the present may properly be asked to sacrifice for generations yet unborn. Though the historic death rate of nations, and especially of political regimes, has been rather high, for a nation's leaders to admit to possible failure of indefinite national survival would only assure an early demise. The belief in an endless future is a necessary, though not sufficient, condition for any future at all.

Man's Place in the Temporal Order

Astrophysicists and other cosmologists are by no means agreed on the history of the universe and its future course. Perhaps the most common view, by no means unchallenged, is that of the "evolutionary" universe, formed into systems and galaxies that are moving apart at high speed. If space is infinite, then time may be also. If space is finite—and here one must suppress the question, and what is beyond?—then the apparent present expansion may decelerate and even reverse directions in "short-term cycles" (a few billion years) of expansion and contraction endlessly repeated.[4] The notions derived from "thermodynamic laws" to the effect that the universe will gradually slow down or that it will end in a "heat death" rest on the assumption of the universe as a closed system and would be inapplicable if, in fact, the universe were an open system.[5]

Not even the age of our own solar system or its prospective destiny is established beyond dispute. Several decades ago the magazine sections of Sunday newspapers carried awesome and pessimistic articles on the gradual cooling of the sun, then thought to be the sole source of our earthly energy, and the eventual certainty of a planet too frigid for habitation if indeed it stayed in its orbit at all. The cooling sun has been placed in some doubt by the theory that nuclear fission and fusion are balanced in a "permanent" equilibrium, and the harnessing of nuclear energy offers some prospect that for a very long period the waning solar energy could be offset by alternative energy sources.

The age of the earth itself is generally placed at around 4.6 billion years.[6] Geologists and paleontologists delight in pointing out the small fraction of that time that any human or humanoid creatures have been on earth and the extremely tiny fraction represented by man's recorded history.

The neurotic earthling would have to be desperate, indeed, for a focus of his anxiety if he were troubled by cosmic evolution, especially in view of the more immediate prospect of man's achieving the earth's destruction without cosmic aid.

It is not just a nuclear holocaust that is threatening, though that threat is real and earnest. Human ingenuity has been used to alter even the physical and biological environment and some of these changes imperil the evolutionary capacity of the human species to adapt to the poisoning of the atmosphere and of food and water. Rachel Carson, noting that over long periods life in general and man in particular have adjusted to hostile elements in the environment, writes: ". . . time is the essential ingredient; but in the modern world there is no time. The rapidity of change and the speed with which new situations are created follow the impetuous and heedless pace of man rather than the deliberate pace of nature." [7]

The "control" of nature, Miss Carson argues, is incomplete and often has lethal consequences, for man is a natural being and cannot finally divorce himself from his evolutionary origins in an earthly environment, despite his arrogant attempts to treat his physical surroundings and fellow inhabitants as enemies to be enslaved or eliminated.

Certain cosmologists of a speculative turn of mind—and what

cosmologist is not?—have begun to ask an extremely disturbing question: once intelligent creatures on any planet capable of supporting life have evolved to the point of the possibility of their own self-destruction, through discovery of the "ultimate" secrets of the universe with respect to matter and energy, does that discovery indeed ensure their termination? [8] This kind of question requires thinking on the grand scale. The way it is put is doubly deflating to man, for it suggests that he is not unique among the intelligent creatures of the universe and that he not only shares individual mortality with all of life but may also share a kind of collective and, indeed, global mortality by his less than godlike capacity for mastery and, crucially, for self-control.

The cosmological assumption of the question is an exercise in probability. Among the many galaxies in addition to our own, the argument goes, the chances are small that the earth in its solar system is unique in providing the minimum essential ingredients for life. Given those conditions, the argument proceeds, the necessary chemical combinations to produce self-perpetuating life probably occur. The natural laws of evolutionary adaption and selection then set in, and one major form of evolutionary success, a high level of intelligence, eventually appears. But, to repeat the question in another way, is this a cycle that is endlessly repeated in space but self-terminating in any particular place?

The question is fascinating in part because in form and in substance it is a scientific one; it is answerable, given some way of studying the history of other inhabited solar satellites. Yet, in view of man's limited individual life, he cannot hope for an answer even for his own petty satellite. If the earth avoids its own destruction, how long must it do so to provide a firm negative answer in one case? And, if it fails to do so, is the outcome to be expected in the grand scheme of things or only an exception in a cosmic statistical distribution?

Individual life expectancies, which might, of course, be lengthened by a few years or a few decades, still set limits on asking questions and getting answers concerning the vast time-space reaches of the cosmos. Both communication and physical travel are limited in velocity to the speed of light, which is one of the few firmly fixed physical limits. Were there intelligent beings on a planet a thousand light-years away, radio communication with them would require a minimum of two thousand years. That is a long time to await an answer, particularly when there is no assurance of a recipient in the first place. Earthly distances are so small that radio communication is virtually "instantaneous." For interstellar communication there is *no* way of getting information on the current state.

The speculations concerning intelligent life in other places in the universe have been pursued further. Suppose, the question goes, that someone were trying to communicate with us, what signal would be used? A natural "physical" frequency, surely, particularly that of hydrogen.[9] Radio telescopes are now being developed to scan the heavens for the 1420-megacycle frequency, and radio signals are being sent out.

The question—is anyone trying to communicate with *us?*—exhibits once more man's arrogance. Unless the hypothetical communicators had advanced to the point of being able to identify the inhabited, or probably inhabited, planets, any communication would be more likely to resemble the foundering ship's SOS or the mythical castaway's bottle-encapsulated message thrown into the sea.

Suppose a signal were received. Would there be any assurance that the long-lived senders or their descendants were patiently waiting an answer? Would a stream of signals that suddenly ceased indicate impatience or confirm the theory that the achievement of a technology sufficient to broadcast messages to the universe would also be a technology to ensure early self-destruction?

There is, of course, a notion of "sequential immortality" imbedded in the idea of sending a message that would be answered a thousand years from now, received by some alert fortieth-generation successor to the scientific experiment.

The theory of relativity itself offers no way around the velocity-limiting speed of light, but it does offer some possibility of extending the life-span of man. The late John von Neumann, one of the world's most eminent mathematicians and theoretical physicists, in 1946 was engaged in a private conversation concerning the implications of nuclear energy for space travel. Travel to the moon or within the solar system he dismissed as offering no theoretical challenge—it was, he said, only an "engineering question." But, said Von Neumann, suppose one wanted to reach a star one hundred light-years distant. Now the maximum velocity for such a trip would be just short of the speed of light—since, he noted, one would want to arrive as mass and not as energy. The trip would then require something more than one hundred years, which, he also noted, is rather long in the life span of an individual. Since one would also want to return, the two-hundred-year round trip is even longer in relation to human life. However, he continued, relativity theory would indicate, and some experimental evidence seems to confirm, that at velocities of such magnitude the vital processes are radically slowed down. One might thus make the trip in two hundred calendar years that would be only, say, twenty years in life-cycle terms. Having captured his audience with this glimpse of relativity theory, Von Neumann was ready for his *theoretically* interesting question: "What," he asked, "happens to my salary in the meantime?"

It seems relatively unlikely that space travel will, in fact, provide a kind of cosmic Shangri-La for substantial numbers of earthlings, but the prospect might well give pause to the comfortable assumptions of actuarial calculators of life expectancies.

Meanwhile, back on earth, man's future is more uncertain and more fraught with visible and invisible hazards than at any time in his short and ambiguous history. In another bit of speculation the same Von Neumann argued that nuclear fission and fusion offered such a potentially limitless source of energy that energy might become a kind of "free good." [10] The earth itself, however, has become too small for this development, he argued, and the power plant should be established on another planet, or on an artificial satellite, where the direct destructive potential and effects of radiation would be reduced.

National states and even some ordinary citizens are now directing at least some efforts toward "buying time," following some constructive as well as merely defensive policies to prevent a catacylsmic destruction and thus to permit the utilization of natural and human resources for human welfare in this and future generations. The key, if it is found, must be essentially political, for it is the representatives of nations with diverse goals and acutely diverse views of how best to achieve them that hold the powers of destruction if not the wisdom to prevent it. Though nuclear warfare might not be *totally* disastrous, as Herman Kahn has argued,[11] its potential destruction of life and property would "at best" be sufficiently great to make the prospect of finding effective and honorable alternatives rather attractive. One might, perhaps, populate a mythical nearby planet with hostile forces and achieve some measure of political integration of the world for common defense. Short of such other-worldly solutions, the question is whether man's historic hourglass is nearing the bottom and cannot be turned over, or are we merely experiencing the special strains attendant on the end of a cycle, which will be followed inexorably by another and another?

NOTES

1. See Arnold S. Feldman and Wilbert E. Moore, "Industralization and Industralism: Convergence and Differentiation," in *Trans. Fifth World Cong. Sociology,* Washington, 1962, Vol. II, pp. 151–169, especially pp. 153–155.
2. See Eyler N. Simpson, *The Ejido: Mexico's Way Out* (Chapel Hill: University of North Carolina Press, 1937).
3. Brandon argues that man's conception of time, but also his attempts to avoid its constraints, are closely linked with religion. See S. G. F. Brandon, *Time and Mankind* (London: Hutchinson, 1951).
4. See *Sci. Am.*, **195**, September 1956, the entire issue of which is devoted to "The Universe." See especially George Gamow, "The Evolutionary Universe," pp. 137–154. For an opposing view see Fred Hoyle, "The Steady-State Universe," pp. 157–166. For a concise review, see Alan Mannion, "An Evolving Universe," *Main Currents in Modern Thought*, **18**, 41–42, November/December 1961.
5. See Richard Schlegel, *Time and the Physical World* (East Lansing: Michigan State University Press, 1961), especially Chapter V, "Time and Our Universe."
6. See John H. Reynolds, "The Age of Elements in the Solar System," *Sci. Am.*, **230**, 171–182, November 1960. See also Harold F. Blum,

Time's Arrow and Evolution (New York: Harper Torchbooks, 1962), Chapter II, "The Chronology of Evolution."

7. Rachel Carson, *Silent Spring* (Boston: Houghton Mifflin, 1962), pp. 6–7.

8. See George W. Boehm, "Are We Being Hailed from Interstellar Space?" *Fortune*, **63**, 145–149, 193–194, March 1961, especially pp. 149 and 193.

9. See Su-Shu Huang, "Life Outside the Solar System," *Sci. Am.*, **202**, 55–63, April 1960; also Boehm, *op. cit.*, p. 193.

10. See John von Neumann, "Can We Survive Technology?" in Editors of Fortune, *The Fabulous Future* (New York: Dutton, 1955).

11. See Herman Kahn, *On Thermonuclear War* (Princeton: Princeton University Press, 1960). See also his *Thinking About the Unthinkable* (New York: Horizon Press, 1962).

Index